KING OF THE GYPSIES

Most gypsies cling to centuries-old taboos and rituals, don't pay taxes and can't read or write. Yet they flourish from coast to coast, drive Cadillacs and Lincoln Continentals, and have turned thievery into an art form.

You will learn how they do it in this irresistible book by the author of *SERPICO* and *THE VALACHI PAPERS*.

"A masterful play-by-play exposé of gypsy violence, revenge, con games, and shams as well as an amazing collection of gypsy folklore . . . Irresistible."

—*Chicago Tribune Book World*

"It's readable, it's dramatic, and, like a novel, it tells the story of an entire people principally through the travail of one of them . . . Maas has captured the gypsy soul."

—*The National Observer*

"Peter Maas has the eye of an experienced journalist and fills his narrative with the kind of detail that makes a good story come alive."

—*The New York Times Book Review*

Dino De Laurentiis Presents
A Frank Pierson Film

KING OF THE GYPSIES

STERLING HAYDEN

JUDD HIRSCH

ANNETTE O'TOOLE

ANNIE POTTS

ERIC ROBERTS

SUSAN SARANDON

BROOKE SHIELDS

SHELLEY WINTERS

Produced by Federico De Laurentiis
Written for the Screen and Directed by Frank Pierson
A Paramount Release

The Motion Picture is suggested by the
book *King of the Gypsies* by Peter Maas

KING
OF THE
GYPSIES

—◦✦◦—

Peter Maas

BANTAM BOOKS
TORONTO · NEW YORK · LONDON

*This low-priced Bantam Book
has been completely reset in a type face
designed for easy reading, and was printed
from new plates. It contains the complete
text of the original hard-cover edition.*
NOT ONE WORD HAS BEEN OMITTED.

KING OF THE GYPSIES

*A Bantam Book | published in association with
Viking Penguin, Inc.*

PRINTING HISTORY

Viking edition published October 1975
2nd printing .. November 1975   3rd printing .. December 1975
4th printing .... February 1976
Literary Guild edition published December 1975
A condensed version appeared in NEW YORK MAGAZINE
September 1974

Bantam edition | June 1976
2nd printing .... June 1976   4th printing .... July 1976
3rd printing .... July 1976   5th printing .... August 1976
6th printing .... December 1978

*Bantam Books are published by Bantam Books, Inc. Its trade-
mark, consisting of the words "Bantam Books" and the por-
trayal of a bantam, is Registered in U.S. Patent and Trademark
Office and in other countries. Marca Registrada. Bantam
Books, Inc., 666 Fifth Avenue, New York, New York 10019.*

PRINTED IN THE UNITED STATES OF AMERICA

CONTENTS

This is in loving memory of Audrey;
and it is also for John Michael

AUTHOR'S NOTE

As a result of some of my previously published work, I receive a steady stream of tips and suggestions about possible projects from friends, acquaintances and total strangers. And that was how I first heard of Steve Tene and the Bimbo tribe of gypsies.

A fellow called me one day, reminded me of how we had been introduced by a mutual friend in a restaurant a few weeks before and said there was this gypsy that a friend of *his* in California had told him about. The gypsy, he said, was someone I might find of interest. As it happened, I had a free afternoon and I met with Steve. I wasn't overly impressed. He seemed vague, and much of what he had to say sounded awfully farfetched to me. Besides, I had just signed a contract for another book, which would be my first effort at fiction, and I was anxious to get started on it.

But when Steve managed to involve me personally in the turbulent and often deadly affairs of the Bimbo tribe, suddenly some of the things he had related did not appear so farfetched any more. And with all the governmental and corporate prying into everybody's personal lives these days, I became fascinated at the thought of so many gypsies (the best part was that nobody really knew how many) living essentially as they had for hundreds of years, blithely escaping the massive surveillance and computerization that has been increasingly bugging the rest of us.

As it turned out, Steve's knowledge was limited to his own experiences, and this was true of almost every gypsy I interviewed. But through him I was able to meet other gypsies, who opened doors to still more gypsies, which cut short an investigative process that normally would have taken years, if, indeed, it could have been done at all.

Even so, it was in many ways the most difficult assignment I have undertaken. During the years when I had been a reporter—looking into miscarriages of justice, crooked business deals, organized crime, corrupt cops and politicians and the like—I could at least fall back on a common ground of word meanings, of aspirations and attitudes, motivations, hopes and fears. But with the gypsies it was a case of culture shock, whether they talked freely to me or I talked them into talking to me. Until I finally learned to accept, for example, how little heed gypsies pay to names, it was impossible for me to comprehend that Steve could have married and lived with a woman for four months without knowing her last name.

Some gypsies I interviewed lied to me outright. Others lied to me without knowing that they were lying, since a number of them are more credulous about their own myths than any outsider could ever be. Most insidious of all were gypsies who sat before me trying to figure out what I wanted to hear and then gravely supplied it. Finally there were the gypsies who told an objective truth, but how was one to know this?

Since gypsies have no written records of their own, an extensive and painstaking investigation had to be conducted wherever documentation might exist—obscure police files, ancient court records and old newspaper clippings in out-of-the-way towns. This search led to other incidents that the gypsies themselves had not recalled. Once I had this material in hand, it also became an invaluable guide in determining which gypsies were telling the truth and which were not.

So, for their help in an often frustrating endeavor, I want particularly to thank my own research assistant, Joan Spano; Dick Connolly of the Boston *Globe;* Shari Hanhardt of the City News Bureau in Chicago; and John Trezevant of Field Enterprises, who may be a big newspaper executive now but who is still a reporter at heart.

PETER MAAS

New York City
June 9, 1975

If you ask twenty gypsies the same question, you will get twenty different answers. On the other hand, if you ask one gypsy the same question twenty times, you will still get twenty different answers.

—Old saying

PART
I

***

The Legacy

He can never forget it, and in the spring of 1974, flying in from Los Angeles to New York on TWA 840, it came to him again, as it always did every time he was being drawn back into the life—that first memory of being a gypsy. He was four years old then and in this jewelry store with his mother, listening to what would become such a familiar litany. She imperiously revealing that she was up from her Brazilian coffee plantation on a buying spree, sneering at the gems in black velvet trays spread out in front of her, demanding to see something better, and suddenly giving him a tremendous whack in the small of the back when the jeweler turned away to oblige her, and as he began to cough reflexively, she crying, "Oh, my precious, what's wrong? Quick, a glass of water for my baby!" and as the water was being brought, pressing the handkerchief to his lips, and before he knew it, the diamond was in his mouth, and then the water, and he had swallowed it. And later, after the police had been summoned and they both had been searched and released, his mother so regally indignant that even the jeweler began muttering confused apologies, he was rushed back to the Henry Street tenement on Manhattan's Lower East Side and deposited naked on a pile of newspapers and fed slice after slice of bread to coat the diamond on its way through his digestive tract, surrounded by the intent, impatient faces of his mother and father, aunts and uncles and older cousins, all coaxing, "Come on, Stevie," until there was a jubilant shout when, finally, he passed the stone, and while it was being cleaned and admired and valued on the spot, he remembered how he wandered around alone chewing on what was left of the bread.

He is now twenty-six, and if he were just another gypsy kid, it would have been a lot easier in the end, on him and everybody else involved. But he is not. His name is Steve Tene, and he is a grandson of King Tene Bimbo, who, before his death in October 1969, was the most powerful of the gypsy chieftains in this country—the "King of Kings," they used to call him, a kind of Mafia-like "Boss of All Bosses." For all their anarchistic ways, gypsies have a profound sense of their own mystique, of their being gypsies, and beyond this a passionate awareness of their tribal identity. Each of the gypsy tribes—or *vitsas* as they are known in Romany, the gypsy language—has a *baro,* or tribal leader; they are, for the most part, amiable if cunning fellows, given to much philosophizing—e.g., "There are lies more believable than truth"—and expert practitioners of a *laissez-faire* approach to life and its manifold problems.

King Tene Bimbo was different. He pursued power relentlessly, for its own sake as well as for the tribute he was able to squeeze out of his subjects; and from about 1905 as a lithe and dapper youth barely out of his teens, through muscular, handlebar-mustached middle age, to the corpulent hulk he had become when he expired at last at the age of eighty-five, he put together a singular career that is recorded in scores of faded newspaper clippings, in bulging files of local and federal law-enforcement agencies and in the constant chatter among gypsies wherever they gather. "If there are any charges that have not been brought against Tene Bimbo, the Gypsy King," the Chicago *Daily News* reported as far back as 1930, "it is probably just an oversight."

To a *gadjo*—anyone who is not a gypsy—Tene Bimbo provided whatever explanation regarding his royal station that he found convenient or thought would work at a given moment. Once he claimed that he had been officially recognized by the United States government as the "King of All Gypsies" because he had personally recruited practically a whole division of his fellow tribesmen into the Army during World War I, an act of patriotism, he further stated, that really turned things around for the Allies. Another time he swore in a court deposition that his "right to the title and exalted position of King of the Gypsies is based upon an ancient ritual and established claims of inheritance covering a period of hundreds of years." This was not only sure-fire for a laugh among gypsies because it wasn't true, since there is no divine right or formal succession for Romany kings, but doubly so because it was just the sort of line that gypsies believe every *gadjo* laps up.

Even gypsies are not immune to fanciful tales of how Tene Bimbo came to be their king—how as a child his wisdom was such that gypsies five times his age would seek his counsel, how in the old caravan days he would move through each night's encampment hewing wood and drawing water for those unable to fend for themselves, how as he grew to maturity he selflessly took from the rich and gave to the poor. But the reality of Tene Bimbo's power was a good deal less poetic. It was built on fear. As a rule gypsies have never been notably violent. If a gypsy transgressed the Romany code, he was judged by a council of tribal elders called a *kris,* and if he was found guilty, his punishment was usually a fine. King Tene Bimbo, however, preferred more direct action. He had the reputation of being a merciless killer, which was further enhanced by his alleged association with Al Capone. Their alliance is supposed to have been cemented when he carried out a Capone contract to assassinate a Chicago cop. According to Detective Eddie Coyne of the New York Police Department, who has been specializing in gypsy affairs for the past twelve years, "We've got that information in our files. I don't know if it's true or not, but the gypsies believe it and that's all that counts."

Aside from the Capone connection, mythical or not, there are any number of verifiable examples of Tene Bimbo's murderous bent. He lived in Chicago for many years, and when an early rival there earned his wrath, he promptly went out and hired a hit man to gun the rival down. Like most gypsies he habitually took to the road, and once, on his way to Boston, displeased by what he considered a lack of proper homage from two other tribal chiefs he had run into, King Tene triggered a shootout that required more than a hundred police officers to quell and had the citizenry of a Massachusetts town on the verge of mass hysteria. Without batting an eye he tried to dispatch still another claimant to his throne in New York by concocting charges against the man that got him a fifteen-to-twenty-one-year sentence in Sing Sing prison. In Philadelphia, enraged when resident gypsies refused his extortion demands and mocked him moreover as a pretender, he led his retinue on a rampage that left two of the locals dead and a third paralyzed for life; having made his point, he then headed for California and continued his reign of terror up and down the West Coast. While the most larcenous gypsy might recoil from such heavy-handed tactics, King Tene on occasion could also display an epic flair for boldness and resourcefulness; nothing makes the Romany heart beat faster than an artfully contrived caper, especially at the expense of the *gadjo,* and there are few on record more dazzling than the escape from custody of his pipe-smoking spouse Queen Mary Bimbo after she had been incarcerated in an Illinois state reformatory—he not only plotted every detail of the escape itself but then made sure that, despite the usual thirteen-state alarm and FBI "wanted" circulars, she remained at liberty for the next eleven years until her death at the age of sixty-two.

For the grandson, Steve Tene, the old man remained basically an abstraction. He heard most of the stories about him, of course, but it was difficult to reconcile them with the childhood memory he had of his grandfather, of sitting in his lap nestled against his enormous paunch, toying with a gold medallion on his watch chain, being treated, he recalled, with exceptional gentleness, yet sensing the massive force of the old man's presence, the deference, bordering on the obsequious,

accorded him by anyone who came near. Later, in
his early teens when he was in trouble, Steve went to
him and again was received kindly, although this time
a sharper, more matter-of-fact air shaped their relationship. But in the end being one of King Tene Bimbo's
grandsons had no specific meaning for him other than
a certain prestige, really a reflected glory. That and a
nickel, as they used to say, could get him a ride on
the New York subway. There were, after all, some
fifty other grandsons kicking around, to say nothing of
seven sons still very much alive. But the old man had
one last surprise, and it came with a deathbed pro-
nouncement that he had bypassed all those sons and
grandsons to bestow on Steve his two most prized personal possessions—the gold medallion he always wore,
the one Steve as a child had so often fingered, which
had been given to him by *his* father, and a huge, ham-
mered-gold ring festooned with golden Mexican pesos
which bore the inscription "Bimbo 1913."

In the tradition-bound, intrigue-filled, elaborately rit-
ualized Romany world, where the norm is that nothing
is what it seems, Tene Bimbo's legacy was shockingly
clear. The ring and the medallion by themselves had
no formal significance, yet they meant everything.
Through this bequest King Tene was calling upon
Steve to succeed him, to become the next king. For
gypsies everywhere, but particularly for those in the
Bimbo tribe—feared, ruthless and, as noted in police
intelligence files, the most "treacherous" of the sixty-
odd gypsy clans roaming the United States today—the
news was unhinging. In the years immediately preced-
ing the old man's demise, Steve Tene had become a
virtual outcast among his own kind. He had not only

rejected, as much as any gypsy can, the codified life style that has enabled his people to preserve a unique, centuries-old closed society no matter what land they traveled or settled in, had, indeed, not only committed the unpardonable act of "Americanizing" himself, but was actively urging other young gypsies to do the same.

The irony was that Steve probably would have done none of this had it not been for his brutalizing father, and that was the second stunning impact of the old man's bequest. There had always been bad blood between Steve and the father—a squat bellicose man encased in steadily expanding layers of fat, who had apparently inherited all of King Tene's viciousness and none of his intelligence—and whatever remote chance there was of peaceful co-existence between them evaporated finally in the father's rage and humiliation when he learned that Steve was getting the medallion and ring. So far, as a result, a furniture-refinishing business that Steve started in southern California has been fire-bombed, and a mysterious explosion has occurred in the home of his American foster parents, with whom he has lived on and off during his struggle to escape the gypsy ways; Steve himself in a frenzied moment has pumped a .38-caliber bullet into his father, trying for the heart but missing; and agents of the father in turn jumped him in a savage knife attack that miraculously did not blind him, leaving instead a mass of ugly scar tissue under the corner of his left eyelid, where one blade-thrust actually slid past the eyeball into the socket itself. All the gypsies say that it is just a question of time before one of them kills the other, and the smart money is on the father.

The wonder was that this deadly clash did not erupt

sooner, but Steve, like every gypsy child, always had
one word relentlessly drummed into his head, and that
word was "respect"—unquestioning respect for all
elders and especially the family head, the father—and
behind that there was the crushing weight of centuries
of tradition reverberating in such constant admonitions
as "This is the way we do things" or "This is our custom." Again, like most gypsy children, he was not
allowed to attend school, nor did he have any social
intercourse with nongypsies until he was twelve years
old, when he finally fled from his family for the first
time. His father was given to sudden, inexplicable
rages, and once, to teach Steve a "lesson," as he said,
he left him alone in an apartment for two days—man-
acled to a radiator, without food, a glass of water just
out of reach. Steve, then perhaps nine, had nobody
except other gypsy kids to compare notes with, and
while he realized that his situation was bad, he could
only conclude that this was the way life was. Even
when he knew better, after he ran away, he was still
filled with ambivalence toward the father as well as
profound feelings of guilt that he was somehow a traitor
to his heritage, and throughout his teens there was this
recurrent, irrational pattern of running away and being
brought back or returning on his own and trying to stick
it out, only to take off once more. When he was eighteen
and sure that he was free of all the old shibboleths, he
received a call from one of his sisters that he must
come immediately, that the father was critically ill, dying, in a Columbus, Ohio, hospital, and he remembered
yelling at her, "All gypsies are crazy—they hate somebody and when he's dying, they forget everything he's
done!" and the sister sobbing back, "Stevie, he's your

father." That night he left for Columbus. He walked
into the hospital room packed with relatives, and the
father, lying in his bed, said to him, "See, you killed
me. You been away all this time and you put me here
with all the aggravation you gave me. I'm dying." Then
he closed his eyes and groaned, as if it were his last
gasp, "I'm going. . . ." Steve's mother and his aunts
and sisters began to wail, and later at the house they
were staying in they started talking about what a good
man the father was and what a lousy son Steve was.
The fact that all that was wrong with the father was
a ruptured hernia which the family had initially con-
strued to be a heart attack seemed to make little
difference, and suddenly two of his aunts and his older
sister went berserk and leaped at Steve, scratching and
pummeling away. He covered his face until they had
exhausted themselves, and wound up staying dutifully
with his parents for a month or so, driving his mother
around while she practiced her con games, chauffeuring
his father to the nearest racetrack, until the gibes and
insults from the father again became too much for him
to stomach.

In all there were eight children, six daughters and
two sons. Steve was the second oldest and the first boy,
born on April 29, 1949. He thinks it was in New
York City, but only because he has been told this,
and since gypsies rarely bother with birth certificates,
it could have been anywhere along the road. In their
seasonal wanderings many gypsies, including a number
of Bimbos, start off on a circuitous route early in the
spring in the Middle West and head east, with most
layovers in cities like Hoboken and Hackensack, New
Jersey, close by two cemeteries they especially favor as

burial grounds, before retiring to the South and winter in Florida. None of this is fixed. Some gypsy tribes meander almost exclusively through the Southwest and along the West Coast. Still others tend to stay in one locality, with occasional forays elsewhere in the country or across the border into Canada.

Steve was about seven when his mother began to use him regularly as a prop in her particular scam. While gypsies by and large work their swindles out of fortune-telling joints, Anna Tene, also known as Anna Bimbo, preferred a different approach. Quite slender, unlike most Romany women, and adept at assuming an aristocratic manner, she would doff whatever costume might make one think "gypsy"—heavy gold ornamentation, the traditional long, swirling skirt, a low-cut blouse— and thus fashionably dressed she would sally forth as a wealthy Brazilian lady who was either the owner of or prospective heiress to a vast coffee plantation. Her targets were large discount toy and appliance outlets; fur, luggage and jewelry stores; wholesale garment and fabric houses; automobile showrooms—any place that might reasonably attract the interest of a woman of means ostensibly isolated much of the time in the middle of a South American jungle, and that also could be expected to have substantial cash on the premises. She would insist on speaking to the manager or proprietor in his office. If he turned out to be a younger man, she cut her visit short. "Never talk to the young ones," she would enjoin Steve's sisters when they grew old enough for training. "They'll try to paw you and date you, and they don't have any goddamn money anyway. Go after the ones with some age, the older and more bald-headed the better, and brush up against them and hold their hands, and they'll get so excited they won't know what the hell they're doing."

Steve's role, to further allay suspicion, was to be an instant charmer—"That's my youngest," she would proudly say—and then he usually remained outside the office his mother had gone into with her intended victim, on guard for any untoward glances or movement by employees around him who might be alerted by a hidden alarm or, worse yet, the sudden appearance of a cop. He was also the excuse for a fast exit if her con game had gone well; she would appear at the door, supposedly to see how he was, and that was his cue to start crying that he had to go to the bathroom. If he happened to be in the office itself, the signal to begin his toilet act was when she scratched her head. He was always at her side, for instance, when she tried her flimflam on an attorney, presenting herself not only as a plantation owner but one who had recently been widowed. She would say that this sad event caused her to realize that it was past time to make provisions for the future, especially for the "little one" —nodding somberly at Steve—and was seizing this opportunity to draw up a will. It wasn't simply her holdings in the United States as well as in Brazil that had prompted her to come to an American attorney, she confided in a low, hesitant voice, it was just that, as much as she hated to say it, Brazilian lawyers were not to be trusted. Depending on her sense of how well this was going over, she sketched out the dimensions of her estate and how she wanted it handled, and then asked how long it would take to prepare the papers and—before the attorney brought it up—how much would it cost? No matter what price he named, she expressed surprise at how small the amount was. A date was set for her to return, at which time the will would be done and she would either write out a check or, as she said she preferred, pay in cash.

After this preamble, she started her stock routine. Rising from her chair, she would say that she appreciated the gracious manner in which she had been received, and that she would like to send the victim a fifty-pound bag of coffee beans from her plantation, and he would generally reply that this wasn't necessary, and she would stiffen slightly and exclaim, "But I want to! It's a gift, you understand, nothing you have to pay for." And he more often than not mumbled something apologetic, that of course the coffee beans were welcome, and she, mollified, would take a couple of steps toward the door before she stopped again and said, "Yes, you have been very kind, and I have decided to give you my Spanish good luck. In my country we have a special blessing, and I was born with the gift to do this."

Her hope was that the victim would say something like "Oh, really, how fascinating," or at least exhibit amused disbelief, but in any event nothing short of bodily throwing Steve's mother out of the office would get rid of her at this point. Whether he had said anything or not, she was already advancing toward the victim, her demeanor changed, in control now, asking for, really demanding, a penny to work her magic— or a nickel or a dime if he didn't have a penny—and a handkerchief, and whipping out one of her own if he did not have that either, and then wrapping the coin in the handkerchief, and making the sign of the cross with it on his forehead and lips and over his heart, gripping his arm lightly with her other hand, saying, "Excuse me for touching you like this, but this is the way I must bless you," getting him used to the distraction of her fluttering fingers.

The penny, she said, would multiply for him in health and in wealth, and she invoked God's grace to bring good luck to the victim in all his endeavors, and then she told him to thrust his hands into his jacket pockets, to take out whatever was in them except money—money did not interest her, she said—and to hold the contents in his upraised palms so she could bless them too, car keys so that he would always drive safely, a pack of cigarettes so that he would not have cancer, an address book so that none of the names in it would ever harm him, anything that he had aside from matches. "Matches I do not bless," she would say. "Fire I do not bless, that's the devil, you understand?"

She would be standing quite close to the victim, her dark eyes fixed on his, the tone of her voice rhythmic, hypnotic, the words repetitive, calling upon God and the spirits to bless this man, "for nothing to happen" to him or his business or his family, and then, almost as an afterthought, she would ask him if he had any pictures of his family, and the critical moment had arrived when he removed his wallet to show her the pictures. She would grasp the wrist of his hand holding the wallet and bless the pictures with the handkerchief and penny, looking all the while to see if there was a wad of bills in the wallet, and if there was, she would suddenly reach in and pull the bills out, making sure that she kept them in plain view, dangling them disdainfully in front of the victim, to reassure him that they were safe. And then she would take the other end of the bills with the hand that had the handkerchief and hold them up so that he could still see them, or rather was under the illusion that he could, since she carefully positioned them just off and under the point of his chin. "You got here one dollar," she would say, "that is a hundred pennies for you to make a hundred dollars, you understand what I mean? Here is ten dollars, that's a thousand pennies for you to make a thousand dollars, you understand?" She would continue to rattle off the denominations of the bills, translating them into a bewildering count of pennies and future growth, and as she did, her fingers would move slightly faster than her words, expertly peeling off first one bill and then another with a fingernail and palming it in the hand holding the handkerchief.

When she was finished, she would calmly give him back the bills that were left, so that the victim himself was busy replacing them in his wallet while she tucked the ones she had hidden under the handkerchief inside her dress. If everything had gone without a hitch thus far—and she would depend on instinct to judge whether the victim had played along good-naturedly with her or had actually been taken in—she would take a crack at any cash he might have in a strongbox or safe by telling him that although she had blessed his personal money, she needed a new dollar, one connected directly with his business, to make it multiply as well and to counter the evil his competitors and other assorted enemies had in store for him. The biggest score Steve can remember his mother pocketing was nine thousand dollars she lifted from a distraught garment manufacturer whose wife and daughter had been killed not long before in a car accident.

While the vision of a big score was never out of her mind, Steve's mother never pushed for it, content always to settle for whatever she could get. And day in and day out for more than thirty years she has practiced her con with consummate skill. In all that time, according to her police file, she has been arrested on only a half-dozen occasions. Twice—in Minneapolis, Minnesota, and Little Rock, Arkansas—she was escorted out of town and warned never to come back. That was the worst punishment to befall her. Invariably she wangled her way out of a jail term, when convicted on charges of "larceny by trick," and escaped with nothing more than probation or a suspended sentence if, indeed, the accusations against her were not dismissed outright. Sometimes when she got to the "Spanish good luck" part of her pitch, a victim would demand to know why it was Spanish, since the language of Brazil, supposedly her native land, was Portuguese, and she would unleash an incomprehensible torrent of Romany curses and walk out. Once Steve asked her why she didn't just say Portuguese good luck, and she said, "What's that?" Other times a victim would count the bills before putting them back in his wallet and accuse her of shortchanging him. If this happened, she immediately dropped the stolen cash on the floor, then would point at the money, berate the man for his clumsiness in handling it and stalk away indignantly. She approached each potential victim with a gypsy's acute sense of preordination, of what will be, will be. When she was rebuffed by one victim, she would try another, and if rebuffed once more, there would be still a third attempt, and again and again, until she succeeded. Her average take on a working day was around two hundred dollars, and she rarely returned home with less than a hundred. And if her own doggedness flagged now and then, there was always the thought of her husband, Steve's father, waiting for her with his unpredictable rages, to spur her on.

The father, except for sporadic extortion plots directed toward other gypsies, liked to while away his days gambling, usually at a racetrack. In police identification sheets he is listed as Ephrem Tene, together with some ten aliases. Among gypsies he is called "Al" or "Big Al," but most often "Carranza." Steve unfailingly calls him Carranza, and I once asked if the name had a special meaning, and Steve replied, "Yes, it means son of a bitch." When I checked this with several other gypsies, they said the same thing. Later I discovered that it meant nothing of the sort, that names in general are a very casual affair with gypsies, that gypsies as a rule have one or more names for the benefit of the *gadjo* world and still others reserved exclusively for gypsy use, and that in fact Steve's grandmother had chosen to call this particular son Carranza purely by happenstance. She had seen a movie featuring an especially villainous Mexican bandit named Carranza and came home that night and said to the son, who had apparently exhibited signs of truculence at an early age, "You're like him, you're Carranza," and the name stuck.

It is a measure of the gypsy mind that when I asked Steve why he had told me that Carranza meant son of a bitch when it didn't, he said, "Well, he *is* a son of a bitch." I launched into a laborious explanation of the difference between meaning something and being something, and as I did, I caught him looking at me as if I had taken leave of my senses.

And now, because of Carranza, Steve Tene was on this flight from Los Angeles to New York to help a younger sister, Sonia, who, sold into marriage against her will for $5,750 when she was fourteen, and at seventeen the mother of a two-year-old daughter and three months pregnant with still another child, had tried to commit suicide after having been beaten up both physically and psychically by Steve's father.

The unreality of it is overwhelming. The year is 1974, and people are watching on color television events taking place halfway around the world, and they have become so blasé that most of them can't remember the name of the last man who walked on the moon, and neon-lit streets are jammed with honking automobiles, and newspapers carry reports of the latest rally of the women's liberation movement. Yet for the gypsies, time stands still, the clock has never moved, and what happened to Sonia could just as easily have occurred a thousand years ago, and Steve instead of arriving on a jet could be galloping in on a horse through some dark and silent forest in Central Europe to save his sister.

But it is here and now in the middle of New York, and despite the grandfather's desire that Steve succeed him, the old-line gypsy power structure, especially in the Bimbo tribe, remains emotionally on the side of the father, Carranza, and Steve has to be very careful wherever he goes. So he checked into an East Side hotel on Lexington Avenue, the Summit, rather than one on the West Side of Manhattan, where he figured the risk of being spotted by an ally of his father's was greater, particularly around the Times Square area. As a further precaution, he registered under the name of Tom Day. Such aliases come naturally to him. He has used so many of them in so many scams and hustles in so many different places that there are often moments when he must stop and think who he is this time. He always chooses single-syllable names that he can learn to sign by rote, since like most gypsies, except for being able to recognize, say, the spelling of a certain city or to take down a telephone number, he is illiterate.

At the Summit Hotel all Steve could think about was the father, and he phoned a Mafia kid he knows and explained why he was in New York, and asked for a gun. "I should of finished him off before, when I had the chance," Steve said. "I'm going to cut his fucking heart out and put it in my mother's hand."

"Hey, listen to me," he recalls the Mafia kid saying. "You blow him away, you're in real trouble. What good's that for your sister?"

"I don't care. The man ain't fit to live, and if you don't do me the favor, I'll get a gun somewhere else."

"So get it, but not from me. That's the favor I'm doing you."

The two argued some more, and Steve finally sighed and said, "All right, I guess you're right."

He had no precise idea where his sister Sonia was at the moment, but he did not doubt that he would find her. The same gypsy network that had informed him of her suicide attempt would work again. He would make some phone calls, move around a little, and then wait, and something would happen. It is an integral part of being a gypsy that even he can never get away from, the day-to-day fatalism that has helped his race sustain itself without a flag, a homeland or a church in country after country since its first recorded trek westward across Asia Minor twelve centuries ago.

While Steve laughs off the carefully nurtured legend of gypsy expertise in curse-removals, astrology, tea-leaf readings and similar paid divinations as a "lot of crap," he still insists that there are a select extrasensory few, among whom he counts himself one, who were born with a "veil over their foreheads," who have the "gift," and shortly after his arrival in New York he encountered, on Fifty-first Street near Second Avenue, what he considered a highly propitious omen. He was walking by a trashcan that held a rolled tapestry of some sort, an irresistible object of curiosity for any gypsy. As he started to examine it, he heard a whimpering inside and discovered that it concealed a quivering, filthy white puppy he guessed to be about three weeks old. Gypsies traditionally have an affinity for animals—Steve himself has a pair of well-trained German shepherds in California —and he immediately wrapped the puppy in newspaper and brought it back to his hotel, stopping off on the way to buy a bowl, milk, dog shampoo and flea powder. He washed the dog with a damp cloth, got the floor maid to fetch a box for it to sleep in and used her to make a connection in the hotel kitchen so that broiled filet mignon was soon being sneaked up on a regular basis for it to eat. Under his care the puppy began to thrive, and Steve at once drew the parallel with his missing sister.

Sonia, at an age when most girls in America are starting high school, had been sold into marital servitude to a gypsy family in Jacksonville, Florida, that traveled the Southern carnival circuit. She was the seventh of the eight brothers and sisters. At the time, Steve had already left home for good and her four older sisters were also married and away. There remained a brother, Tommy, who drove for the mother on her rounds, and another sister, four years younger. At best Sonia's childhood had been ephemeral. She can recall a Raggedy Ann doll and an occasional game of hopscotch, but like Steve she was not allowed to play with American children nor was she permitted to go to school, except for a brief, two-month period in Cleveland when she was about ten. Even this required the reluctant connivance of her mother, after much tearful pleading on Sonia's part. Sonia would slip out of the house at six-thirty in the morning before her father was awake and then would sit in front of a nearby public school until it opened for classes. Her father thought she was out early selling flowers or begging, a daily task she was first sent into the street to perform when she was eight. He began grumbling when the amount of money she brought home at night dropped off, despite her frantic efforts to make up for lost time once school was over, and her education was abruptly terminated, complete with a beating, when the father finally caught her doing homework. After that she was placed under strict supervision. An older sister and some cousins were assigned to teach her more sophisticated thievery. Sonia was never able to develop much of a knack in picking pockets, but she displayed an instinctive talent for fortune-telling which made her an attractive buy for the carnival family.

In trying to help her now, Steve was driven by a special guilt. The week before her marriage Sonia had appealed to him to do something to prevent it, and he in effect had done nothing. He was living in Los Angeles then, and he simply told her that if she wanted to, she could come and stay with him. But she was too young and too afraid of the father, of what he might do to her and to Steve if she did not accede to his wishes. "Marry the boy," her mother counseled. "You'll have a good home and you'll be happy. You'll learn to love him."

She could not abide either the boy, two years her senior, or her in-laws, but in the end she had no recourse. The fact that she was underage meant nothing. Gypsy marriages are conducted solely within the Romany community without benefit of any religious or civil sanctions. Worse yet for her was the carnival existence she had to endure. Traveling was no novelty, for her own family was constantly on the move, but it had always been from city to city. She was an urban gypsy, used to apartment or storefront living, and suddenly she found herself living on the outskirts of small Southern towns in a cramped, decrepit trailer, cooking over portable kerosene stoves or open fires, washing clothes and bathing in plastic tubs, hot water at a premium, toilet facilities wherever she could find them. As the newest female member of the family, despite her quick pregnancy she not only had to cook, clean and wash for her husband, his two brothers, his mother and father and a sister-in-law with tenure, but also was required, of course, to work a fortune-telling tent. When she could not take it any longer, she fled home with her baby girl. "If I got to be married," she told her father, "I want my own place. I want to live my way." But Carranza, faced with the prospect under gypsy law of having to repay at least half of her purchase price, together with losing "respect" because of not being able to control his daughter, forced Sonia to return, after exacting a promise from the carnival gypsies that they would "treat her right."

Nothing really changed, however, and Sonia eventually ran away again, this time with another gypsy boy by whom she became pregnant once more. They went to live with the boy's parents, who were a revelation to her, a timorous, poor couple who treated her with a kindness she had never known. For the first time in her life she went out scouring for money, not because she had to but because she wanted to, and to make ends meet as her pregnancy advanced, the boy got a job doing body-and-fender work.

Her father finally tracked them down in Philadelphia. Sonia received a telephoned warning from a friend, and she and the boy left on the run, leaving her daughter behind with the boy's parents. When Carranza invaded their apartment, he demanded ten thousand dollars or Sonia's return. They replied that the best they could do was a thousand dollars, with perhaps another five hundred later on. Carranza sneered at the offer and took Sonia's daughter with him—after so terrorizing the boy's parents, threatening to have them "locked up" on kidnapping charges, that they also left town. Sonia and the boy were hiding in Baltimore when they heard what had happened, and she called her father to beg him to let her lead her own life. "I'm not going to let that kid fuck you for nothing," he bellowed. "You're not going to have your way. I'm going to spend whatever it takes to get you two, and I'm going to break that bastard's legs, and I'm going to have his mother and father locked up. I'm going to have everybody locked up that's involved with you, that's helping you. I curse my dead mother and my dead father if I don't do this."

It was the last threat, as serious an oath as a gypsy can make, that caused the boy to lose his nerve and desert Sonia. "The father was feared," he explained later. "He wasn't kidding, you know what I mean, and he was too strong. He had this reputation of having people locked up and having them beat up, hiring people to beat them up bad, and I was afraid, you know, like for my mother and father. Their health wasn't so good anyway."

Sonia made one final attempt to placate Carranza. She knew that what infuriated him now was not so much having to give back part of her marital price to the carnival family—he could deny any claims on that count because she had been so badly abused by them—but that given her present circumstances he could not arrange a decent resale to another gypsy family. So she went to the rented house in New Jersey, near Hackensack, where he was then living, and said, "Leave my life alone. It's true I don't have no money to give you today. But take the fifteen hundred his people offered, and wait till I make money, me and him, and we'll give it to you, whatever you want. Just give us some time." At first the father agreed, with the proviso that Sonia's daughter stay with him as a hostage. When she protested, he suddenly changed his mind again and warned that if it came down to it, he would return her to her husband. "You think he's so good, *you* live with him," she screamed, *"you* take his shit!" For a week or so, hoping to reverse things, she stayed in New Jersey with Carranza and submitted to a relentless barrage of curses and progressively severe thrashings, until in desperation she grabbed a bottle of tranquilizers and swallowed them all. Her mother called the police, and she was rushed unconscious to a hospital where her stomach was pumped out and where she apparently was still being held.

By now Steve had learned most of this, but what he did not yet know was the name of the hospital.

As a result of his tension-filled life, Steve Tene has for several years periodically endured agonizing ulcer attacks, and in New York, worrying about Sonia and drinking too much because of this, he felt the ulcer starting to kick up once more. To see him, however, you would never know it. He moves with animal grace, his manner deceptively relaxed, his voice always soft. He is very confident of his looks and will recount with disarming innocence how a girl he picked up told him, "Wow, you are one handsome guy." A well-proportioned five-feet-nine, he has thick dark-brown hair, clear skin, luminous black eyes, and a luxuriant mustache. He bears a striking resemblance to the actor Omar Sharif, and more often than not some girl will remark about this, and Steve, to get things going, will say, "Oh, do you really think so? I guess that's because I'm his son."

One night, in his restless prowls around the city, waiting for some definitive word of his sister's whereabouts, he walked into an ugly reminder of his own past. Not far from the Summit Hotel, on Third Avenue between Fifty-third and Fifty-fourth Streets, there is a stretch of sidewalk called the "meat rack," where boys, mostly teen-agers, line up for the East Side carriage trade. A lot of them started out as "chickens," runaway waifs preyed upon by homosexual hawks. Steve was once a chicken. It began with a bloodcurdling experience in Philadelphia at the age of twelve that still makes his voice tremble when he talks about it. After a morning out shining shoes, he had returned home to find Carranza in one of his rages storming around the apartment. He had just put down the money he had earned when his father suddenly turned on him and demanded that he have sex with his mother. "Go on," he yelled, "it'll make a man of you." Horrified when he realized that his father was serious, Steve jumped out of a second-story window, his fall luckily broken by clothesline in the yard below. "It was crazy, sick," he says. "My mother was standing there saying nothing, like she was going to go along with it. They'd been fighting all week and, I don't know, maybe she was getting even with him for the things he'd been taking out on her, and would hold this over his head, and shame him in front of all the other gypsies."

Steve scrambled out of the yard, begged enough change to buy a batch of newspapers wholesale and

then resold them in bars and restaurants, cadging a little extra whenever he could, until he had enough for
bus fare to New York, where his grandfather was supposed to be staying somewhere in the West Eighties.
He arrived in Manhattan late that evening and began
trudging up Broadway. He got as far as Seventy-second
Street when a young man fell in step with him and
asked him where he was going. Steve explained that he
was searching for his grandfather, and the young man
said, "Where are you from?"

"From Philadelphia, I ran away from home."

"Yeah, how old are you?"

"Sixteen," Steve lied.

The young man asked him if he was hungry and
offered to buy him something to eat. Steve, who had
only a quarter left, accepted. Over hamburgers in a
coffee shop, the young man said his name was José, and
while they were eating, two other men joined them.
One was called Eddie, the other Chuck. Then José
asked Steve if he was "gay," and Steve, under the im-
pression that gay meant lively, said yes, and José said
there was this party that Steve would enjoy and that
afterward he would help him look for his grandfather.

The party, he recalls, was in a basement apartment.
There were a number of men there, and some women.
The man he knew as Eddie proffered a cigarette, and
Steve refused. "Come on, have one," Eddie said.
"You're old enough." And Steve said, "Well, I ain't
used to it. If I smoked at home, I would get killed."
He took the cigarette finally and also his first drink,
mixed with Coca-Cola. Music was blaring, and José
and Eddie were seated on either side of him, and Chuck
was giving him another drink, and some of the men

and women were dancing, and he was getting dizzy, and the last thing he remembers was that one of the women started taking off her clothes, and then he saw that the woman was a man.

He doesn't know how long he was held captive, perhaps a week. Suddenly one day he sensed that he could go, and he did. As he went out the door, the man called Eddie laughed and said, "So long, gypsy boy." He left with the discovery that he had something to sell that some men would buy, and for the next year and a half that was basically how he lived. He spent a couple of days panhandling and sleeping in hallways at night, gravitating to Forty-second Street, where other chickens explained to him where and how to stand and what the going rate was. "Don't be afraid," he was told. "Tell the guy you want twenty, and if he doesn't have twenty, ask for ten, but don't go for less than ten." Steve did not look further for the grandfather, certain that his father had contacted the old man by this time and poisoned his mind against him. Occasionally he attempted to break away from the street life. On his thirteenth birthday he went into a Catholic church, and in the confessional he told a priest the trouble he was in and asked what he should do, and the priest advised him to go home, which was the one thing he would not do. For a while he had a dish-washing job in a hash house in Greenwich Village but was fired when he refused to be the aggressor in a homosexual affair with the manager. He had been staying in a succession of rented rooms, but he had become friendly with a lesbian who worked as a prostitute and who used to stop in the restaurant at night, and she invited him to move in with her, and through her he was introduced to pills, uppers and downers. That was finished, however, when the lesbian brought in a permanent girl friend, a secretary in a law firm, and one night, sleeping in the living room, he heard them fighting and the secretary was saying, "You know we can get busted for that goddamn gypsy, he's a runaway, and if his parents ever get ahold of us, we've had it, baby, you know it," and the next day he left.

He also tried stealing, which he was not very good at. One afternoon he lifted some rings in a jewelry store, but before he could get out, he was cornered by the young woman working there, a sexy, slightly overweight brunette in her late twenties who was studying to be a painter. Steve stared at her with his dark eyes and spilled out his whole traumatic story, and the desperate straits he was in, as fast as he could, topping it off with the revelation that he was a gypsy. Whether he perceived it or not, he could not have picked a better audience. The woman was an incurable romantic, and she wound up telling him that he could stay at her place for a few days. The second night he was there he went to bed with her, and she proposed an arrangement whereby he could remain as long as he liked in return for cleaning her apartment and posing for her as a model. While he was with her, he got another job as an apprentice refinisher in an antique shop on Third Avenue. He enjoyed the work, but it lasted little more than two months. He remembers the exact day it ended—the day President Kennedy was assassinated. When the news came over the radio, the elderly lady who owned the shop had a heart attack and died, and her son closed the business. Afterward Steve reverted more and more to his chicken ways. Living in the woman's apartment became awkward—she had a life and lovers of her own—and he disappeared with increasing frequency for days on end, and then one inevitable night he was spotted standing in a doorway on Forty-second Street by members of the Bimbo tribe and was returned to his family.

Over the years, however, he has remained in touch with the woman, and when I went to see her, she was in the same apartment, unmarried, in her early forties, heavier but still striking, and still painting. She told me that when she first grabbed Steve trying to make off with the rings in the jewelry store, he reminded her of a wild animal. As she spoke, two mongrel dogs kept jumping up on my lap. They were strays she had found in the street and taken in. She laughed nervously. "You're a week late," she said. "I had a cat I was trying to find a home for, but I got one." There was a muted cooing in the background. It was coming from a pigeon in her bedroom. She had seen it fluttering around helplessly on the sidewalk, a wing broken, and she had brought it home. On the walls of the apartment, along with other paintings, were several portraits of Steve as a thirteen-year-old, heads and full-length nudes. She said that yes, they had slept together, but just once. "The whole thing didn't make sense," she said. "I knew that. He was here, and then he wasn't. Money was a big thing with him, and he had to have it. What did he spend it on? I don't know, clothes mostly and God knows what else." She said that after his relatives had seized him, he would call every so often and ask for money, and the first two or three times she had sent it, but finally she stopped. He would continue to call and ask again, and when she refused, he would drop the subject, as if it had never been broached, and chat on about what he was doing. "He's a gypsy," she said. "What else can I tell you?"

Steve speaks of that time as a chicken in the doorways of New York with a dispassionate shrug. "I didn't like it," he says, "but I had to survive. I didn't do anything myself. I was, you know, passive. I just shut my eyes."

Now, as Steve stood there on Third Avenue twelve years later, remembering it all, dressed in flared chinos, an open-necked shirt and a fringed suede vest, his California tan contrasting sharply with the blank, white faces of the boys leaning against the shop windows along the block, a man came up to him. The man was middle-aged. He was dressed in a conservatively cut gray suit, he carried an attaché case and he was wearing a wedding ring. He was the kind of man you see striding briskly across Grand Central Terminal at the end of a business day on his way to the 5:19 suburban train. "Are you straight or gay?" the man asked.

"Straight."

The man appeared disappointed. He looked at the line-up of waiting boys and then up and down at Steve again, and finally he said, "I'll give you ten dollars for every inch you've got."

"You don't have enough money," Steve said, turning away, the man following him for another half block, attempting to negotiate further, before he gave up.

Steve's own life has been so marked by paradox that it was almost meaningless to him that within an hour after the incident on Third Avenue, a blond woman with a pinched, strained face at an adjoining table in the Summit Hotel bar started talking to him. She had on a purple dress with too many ruffles in it. She said she was a German tourist from Frankfurt. The woman spoke about how lonely she was in New York, and after buying Steve a few drinks she invited him to her room.

"No, I've got too much going on in my head," he said, but she persisted and then said, "I'll give you fifty dollars," and he shrugged and said, "All right."

In one respect Steve had erred in thinking that he could avoid gypsies by staying on the East Side. They seemed to be all over. Within a few minutes by foot from his hotel, around First and Second Avenues, he noted six different *ofisas*—gypsy fortune-telling joints where the age-old *boojo,* or money-switching game, is practiced on gullible persons who have been convinced that they are cursed by unclean cash. Each *ofisa* was marked by a red-and-green neon "Reader and Advisor" sign, usually in a second-story window. Years ago in New York they all were in ground-floor storefronts, and occasionally one still is despite a municipal ordinance which specifically forbids storefronts doubling as living quarters. The ordinance was passed in the early 1940s on orders of Mayor Fiorello La Guardia. When one of the mayor's legal aides noted that it would be particularly hard on gypsies, La Guardia replied, "Good!" The mayor had a personal reason for his bitterness. His first wife, while pregnant, had wandered into a gypsy fortune-telling tent at a fair. The session did not go well, the gypsy woman spitting out a prediction that both Mrs. La Guardia and her baby were doomed to an early death. Mrs. La Guardia was greatly upset by the encounter, and, as it turned out, the child, sickly from birth, contracted tuberculosis and lived less than a year. Mrs. La Guardia also had the disease and died several months later, and Mayor La Guardia was convinced that his wife's will to live was greatly weakened by what the gypsy woman had said.

What has remained inviolate, however, no matter what floor an *ofisa* is on, is that, in accordance with gypsy law, each is separated from the other by at least three city blocks. The New York police conduct an annual precinct-by-precinct survey of these *ofisas* in an effort to monitor gypsy activity in the city, but nobody really knows how many there are at any given moment. The amazing thing is that, except for police files and some welfare rolls, gypsies do not officially exist in the United States. They are not to be found, for instance, in census or immigration statistics, although the best guesses of the current gypsy population in America range from at least 250,000 to as many as a million or more.

Birth control as well as abortion among gypsies is almost unheard of, and some idea of their proliferation can be measured merely by starting with Steve's paternal grandparents. King Tene Bimbo and his wife Queen Mary had fourteen children. They in turn produced seventy-six grandchildren. The grandchildren, many of them still in their teens and twenties, have already produced a hundred and eighty-three offspring of their own and are still counting.

To complicate matters even more, gypsies are constantly on the move. Asking a gypsy where he has been during the past year is like going out to a busy metropolitan airport and spending a couple of hours listening to the destination announcements of departing flights.

And in an era when the invasion of one's privacy is reaching epic proportions and has become a major political issue in this country, with computers routinely folding, spindling and mutilating the average citizen, and data banks bulging with details about his financial status, medical history, sexual habits, and thoughts while shaving, the gypsies remain totally untouched, as invisible on the old print-out as a breeze meandering across the landscape.

No gypsy likes to be pinned down on anything. Real birth certificates, for example, are anathema to him. If he needs a passport or otherwise requires proof of date and place of birth, he will obtain an affidavit for this purpose supplied and sworn to by other gypsies, or he will get a "delayed" certificate of birth one way or another from a cooperative doctor or midwife. The main thing is to be flexible about such matters, since he never knows what kind of potential bureaucratic booby trap lies in wait for him, and he always operates on the theory that it is best to expect the worst. Being inducted into military service was to be avoided at all costs, and it generally was unless a massive, highly motivated investigation took place. Now and then this did occur, and one luckless target was an older cousin of Steve's named John Tene Bimbo, who was indicted in New York at the end of World War II for failure to register for the draft. His defense was that he was underage at the time. Unfortunately for John Tene, the prosecutor in the case was Florence Shientag, an assistant United States attorney who also happened to be Mayor La Guardia's former legal aide, the same one to whom he had confided the story of his first wife's harrowing experience with a gypsy fortune-teller. Mrs. Shientag

spent weeks in Chicago, where John Tene claimed he
was born, and elsewhere, checking obscure records and
unraveling a maze of contradictory material involving
the defendant. King Tene Bimbo himself attended the
trial in New York in 1946. His grandson's contention
was that he had actually been born on October 20,
1928, four years later than the government charged,
and he presented a delayed birth certificate signed by a
Chicago doctor to back him up. Mrs. Shientag produced evidence, based partially on Chicago welfare
records, that he actually had been born in 1924 in
Tennessee. His mother, Bessie Bimbo, known as Pearsa
among the gypsies, clad in a flowing blue and gold
gown and headdress, complete with long gold earrings,
took the stand on behalf of her son. "The same as I
know I got five fingers," she declared, "I know my son
was born on October 20, a Saturday night in 1928, in
Chicago." The reason she had given Chicago welfare
authorities an earlier birth date for her son, she explained, was just a white lie to get a higher relief al-
lowance. When Mrs. Shientag, cross-examining the
witness, suggested that in view of some rambling statements in her testimony, she might not be in complete
"control" of her faculties, Bessie Bimbo rolled with the
punch. "You mean I am crazy?" she said. "My husband always calls me crazy. I don't know why. I got a
good head on my shoulders." But what did John Tene
in was an admission from the doctor that he had been
"misled" into signing the birth certificate for him. The
jury deliberated fifteen minutes before rendering a
guilty verdict, and he was sentenced to two years in
prison. He served about a third of his term, and later
sought out Mrs. Shientag and cheerily told her that it

was the best thing that ever happened to him, that while behind bars he had learned to read and write.

In thwarting the great computer numbers game that pigeonholes the rest of us, any self-respecting gypsy carries at least three social security cards, a handful of drivers licenses and a revolving collection of credit cards in a variety of names. If a gypsy is arrested, which is often the case, he rarely spends much time in jail; if necessary, he makes bail and disappears. Cadillacs and Lincolns, however acquired, are his favorite mode of ground transportation, and an obliging, no-questions-asked state like Alabama promptly mails him his plates and registration papers upon receipt of a money order. If, for some reason, a gypsy desires to travel by plane, he calls an airline, picks a departure date a week or so hence, supplies a phone number and address, asks that the ticket be mailed to him and advises that he will post back a check. When the ticket arrives, protectively, if inadequately, stamped "nonrefundable," the gypsy immediately heads for the airport. He explains at the ticket counter that he has suddenly had to change his schedule, succeeds in changing the reservation and takes off. As in every gypsy hustle, the execution is all-important. To allay suspicion in ordering airline tickets, a round trip is always requested, and a gypsy will earnestly explore with an airline reservations agent the various excursion fares, family plans and day versus night flight prices before, with seeming resignation, he settles on regular first-class accommodations.

Steve showed me how easy it was. He called an airline on my phone and said he wanted to make a reservation for two—for himself and his wife—to Hawaii.

The reservations agent asked when he wanted to leave.

"The tenth of May," Steve said. "In the morning."

"What class, sir?"

"First, please."

After a moment the girl said that first class was full on that date. "How about the eleventh? First class is open on the eleventh."

He hesitated, as if this were something of import to consider, and then said, "All right," and she supplied the flight details and asked for a name and phone number, and after he had given them to her, he said that he might as well make return reservations and wanted to know how much the tickets would cost.

She asked how long he would be staying, and he replied, "About a month," and she said, "Less than thirty days?" and he said, "Yes," and she said in that case he was eligible for the excursion fare. Then she came back on the line apologetically and said that the excursion fare applied only to coach tickets. "Why don't you go coach?" she said. "You'll save a lot of money."

It was just the sort of opening Steve was waiting for. "You know," he sighed, "I should of married a girl like you," and she laughed delightedly. He paused, as though in regretful contemplation of what might have been, before he added, "No, better make it first. You're right, but it's my wife. She really won't go any other way."

The agent's voice was full of warmth and understanding while she tied up the routine loose ends. Would he pick up the tickets? He said no, that he wanted them mailed, and gave my address, and when she asked what form of payment he would use—credit card or check—he said he would mail a check, and that was it. The tickets arrived the next day, and before I sent them back, Steve looked at them wistfully and said, "It's too bad. I've never been to Hawaii."

Since gypsies for the most part are illiterate, a telephone is a crucial means of communication when they move into a new city. To get a phone installed promptly, they will claim an emergency situation of some kind, such as a seriously ill child, and if required will produce a "to whom it may concern" letter from a physician they have bribed along the way. A deposit is of course to be avoided under any circumstances, and to establish a solid community standing, gypsies invariably tell a company service representative that they own the home or apartment in which the phone is to be installed. When asked for the telephone numbers of a close relative and a personal friend as references, they either make them up or tick off ones picked at random from a directory. Occasionally the telephone company conducts a thorough investigation, and an application is turned down. When this happens, a gypsy just dismisses it as momentary bad luck and starts the process all over again using a different name. An added fillip is to have the phone listed under a business heading, such as "John's Roofing Company, Inc." or "Mary's Dress Shop." This not only reinforces an aura of respectability but also enables a gypsy to obtain local credit during his stay in town. And once more Steve demonstrated how simple the procedure is. He got a phone listing for a fake roofing company. Then he applied for various charge accounts, presenting himself as an employee of the firm currently earning two hundred and fifty dollars a week. The fact that he could not write and had to have the credit forms filled out for him only added to his credibility. As he told me, "They just sit there putting down what I tell them, and they're thinking, well, what do you expect, the guy's just a roofer, but he's holding down a regular job," and in the next few days he sat back taking calls from credit agencies as well as individual stores, solemnly verifying all the information that he himself had supplied.

One afternoon, while Steve was still waiting for some further news about his sister Sonia, he and I were walking down Fifth Avenue. In front of Tiffany's there were two beautiful, dark-skinned, big-eyed children, a boy and a girl, possibly ten or eleven years old, each holding carnations and soliciting passersby, "Please buy a flower for the American Indians." I had passed children doing this before, and without really thinking about it, I guess, I had assumed that they actually were Indians.

I learned differently when Steve went over and conversed with them in Romany. After he came back, I asked, "What are they, a brother and sister?"

"No," he said, "they're married. They haven't made love yet, but they're married. She told me his people paid four thousand dollars for her. She's very proud of it."

I knew that, with rare exceptions, gypsy women brought in all the money, and that the price for a wife depended not on her looks but on her earning potential. So I asked him how they could decide on the worth of a girl who was that young.

"Well, they probably figured she comes from a line of good stealers. That's how it usually works. And look, she is good. See that guy she just got a dollar from? She got the dollar and she talked him out of the flower

too, so she can use it again. She told me she already
made thirty-eight dollars today."

"Does this happen often, marrying them off at that
age?"

"Sure," he said. "It happens all the time. It's sad,
isn't it? That's some life those kids are going to have."

Steve asked me to keep walking with him a while
longer. "It's my nerves," he said. "If I don't hear something about Sonia soon, the hell with it, I'll just go
after Carranza myself."

Almost without realizing it, we were on the West
Side of Manhattan, going by the bus terminal on Forty-
first Street, when a voice cried, "Stevie, hey, Stevie!" He
turned and was embraced excitedly by a girl with a
tough sexiness about her who was wearing platform
shoes, tight denim slacks and a denim jacket. She was
a twenty-one-year-old gypsy named Yana, and she had
known Steve Tene for a long time. "What are you doing
here?" she asked. "I thought you was in California."

"Sonia. You heard what Carranza did to Sonia?"

"Yes, I heard about that."

"They got her in some hospital, I don't know, some-
place over in Jersey. Can you help me find out
where?"

"I'll find out. I hate all those goddamn Bimbos, except you."

We went with her to two furnished rooms she had in
a walk-up on Fifty-fourth Street off Eighth Avenue.
She picked up her children, a boy, five, and a girl,
three, whom she had left in the care of a neighbor, and
then made us glasses of tea, so laced with spices and
fruit that it tasted like punch. Even though it was quite
late by now, the boy and the girl sat watching tele-

vision, showing no signs of going to bed. "Well, you know," Steve said, "they're gypsy children."

Yana had married into the Bimbo tribe. But she had grown tired of the constant beatings. The final straw came when her father-in-law drunkenly attempted to sleep with her, and she walked out with her son and daughter. "Let them try and do something about it," she said.

When they were kids, Steve used to drive for Yana and one of his sisters. Gypsy girls start out stealing young. Steve, for that matter, was driving when he was barely eleven. In Chicago, where they were living at the time, his father bribed a state motor-vehicle official and came home one day with an Illinois license certifying that Steve was sixteen. The father wired blocks to the clutch and brake pedals and told Steve to get behind the wheel. While he had observed all the mechanics of driving, this was his initial experience actually doing it. His first, and only, lesson began right in the street, and as Steve pulled away from the curb with a jerk, he bumped into the automobile parked in front of him. There was a man in it, but Carranza leaped out and hurled such a volley of obscenities at him that, apparently cowed, he drove off without a word. Steve recalls how his father sat next to him munching an enormous sandwich in one hand while swatting him with the other every time he made a mistake until, out of self-preservation, Steve managed to gain his grudging approval.

When the girls were stealing, they usually worked in pairs. Steve would cruise past lawns in a residential neighborhood, looking for a likely prospect, preferably an elderly man. If all else failed, the girls knocked blindly on doors until the right one opened. The idea was to get into the house or apartment. Full of wide-eyed innocence, they showed the man a vial and told him that a priest had sent them to deliver holy water to an ill parishioner, but they had lost the address and could they please check his phone book? Sometimes, to gauge the susceptibility of their victim and to worm their way more into his confidence, they would vaguely describe the mythical person they were seeking, and often the victim would say, "Oh, yes, I think I know who you mean. I've seen him around here." After they were inside, one girl would preoccupy the man, flirting with him if that seemed best, or prattling on about all the evil and sickness abounding in the world, while her partner, on the pretense of using the bathroom, raced through the other rooms looking for cash. People always kept money in the same places—under kitchen coffee cans, in closet hatboxes, under beds, beneath clothes folded in a drawer. Once, in Boston, Yana was at her wit's end in an upstairs bedroom when, for no reason she can explain, she stuck her hand in a wastepaper basket filled with trash and at the bottom of it she discovered a metal box. The box was locked, which stymied her for a second, but she was wearing a long skirt, so she finally tucked the box between her legs and waddled out with it. When they broke it open in the car, there were more than five thousand dollars inside.

Giggling over this, Yana re-enacted the shuffle she employed in getting out of the house with the box and then began reminiscing about an accident case Steve had "made" in a Midwestern supermarket. He was already trying to break free from the traditional gypsy life when he and Yana walked into the market, and she saw the broken carton of eggs on the floor and said, "Go ahead," and he said, "No, I don't want to."

"Listen," she said, "God put those eggs there. If you don't do it, I'll shove you myself," and at last he said, "All right, but wait till I take my coat off. I just bought this suit." He went into his routine, she screamed and became a witness, and he was rushed by ambulance to a hospital. He spent three weeks there, so successfully feigning madness as a result of the supposed injury to his head, once hurling a trayful of food at a nurse during a visit from an insurance adjuster, that the company was delighted to settle for twenty-three thousand dollars.

Gypsies are constantly involved in fake accident cases, but Steve was an acknowledged master of the art. At Yana's urging he demonstrated his technique, tossing a pencil on her floor as a prop, slipping on it and flying up in the air. He came down with a tremendous thud and lay so motionless, except for a twitching leg, that I was convinced that he had overdone it and injured himself seriously. Suddenly, as I started toward him, he sat up, beaming; I had reacted exactly as a supermarket manager would have.

Like most gypsies, Steve launched this phase of his career with on-the-job training. He was about sixteen, and on his own, when a cousin came to him one day and said, "You want to make some fast money?"

"Sure. How?"

"It's a cinch."

"Can you get arrested?"

"No, I'm telling you it's easy. Don't worry. Anyway

you're not with your family now and you need the money."

"What do I do?"

"You just walk into this store I know and fall down on something and don't move. Just say you're hurt and groan. We split the settlement fifty-fifty because it's my store, I found it, and I know the insurance company and how they operate because I done business with them before. You just lay there, and they'll call an ambulance. Just remember to tell the insurance adjuster when he comes that a lawyer wants you to sign up with him. And the adjuster will say don't sign with nobody because they will take a third of what you get. The adjuster will say if you don't sign, he will make you an offer, and you just hold out for a little more. I'll be there, helping you."

The cousin went into the store with him. Steve filled a cart with groceries, and then the cousin pointed to a wet spot on the floor and said, "There's the place." An ambulance took Steve to Roosevelt Hospital in New York. The settlement, as he remembers, was with Travelers Insurance for twenty-five hundred dollars. That first time, not knowing how to fall then, he had given himself a nasty knock on the head and actually suffered a mild concussion.

Aside from the acrobatic excellence and acting ability in accident cases that he subsequently developed, Steve had a further advantage. In his days as a chicken, he had met a homosexual doctor, and now he sought him out for coaching on what to expect and how to behave during examinations for his alleged injuries. His best bets, the doctor told him, were headaches, loss of balance and severe back pains. One of the first things that would happen to him, Steve was advised, was that he would be asked to stretch out his arms, close his eyes and touch his nose with the forefinger of his right and left hands. When he tried to do this, he was to start toppling over, always to the same side. He would then probably be told to lean forward slightly, relaxing his body, and attempt to touch his left foot with his right hand and his right foot with his left. From the beginning, Steve was to pretend pain, and then cry out sharply the second he actually started to bend. At some point, the doctor said, he would be asked to lie down on an examining table, and when he did this, he must always remember to get on and off the table slowly and cautiously, and to keep a hand pressed against the small of his back to show how excruciating this move was for him. Once on the table, he would be asked to bend, say, his right knee and then straighten it out. When he tried this, he was to scream in agony. If the examining physician tried to bend it for him, he was to scream again. His doctor friend warned Steve that in a real back injury the pain localized itself after a few days, so he would have to be prepared to select a specific spot for it instead of continuing to say that it hurt all over. If, for example, he elected the right side as the point of pain, he was to allow his left leg to be bent back almost all the way before he yelled. Steve was instructed about other twisting and turning tests and also how the soles of his feet and his legs would be scraped or would have pins stuck in them to measure his reflexes. In such instances, he would simply have to stiffen his body and take it, but he found this remarkably easy once he knew it was coming. Regarding

X-rays and spinal taps, the doctor showed him how to react with such pain that he could not be properly positioned for photographs, and he told Steve, "If they try to give you a spinal, just play dumb and ask what it is. They'll tell you that it's a needle. You ask if it's a big needle and if it will hurt, and they'll have to say yes. You say that you can't stand any more pain, and they won't take a chance trying it."

Steve practiced his groans and yelps and body movements by the hour and became so adept at faking injuries that in San Francisco a doctor brought in by the insurance company actually counseled him not to settle his claim. "You're really hurt," the doctor said. "Wait six months and see what happens. We'll pay the bills. You may be permanently damaged."

Now, on the floor of Yana's apartment where he still sat after his spectacular flip in the air, Steve abruptly stopped smiling, as if embarrassed by this impulsive return to his old life. He quietly asked her what she had been doing. She hesitated, affected by his change in mood, before she said that she was on welfare. As it turned out, she was being quite modest. She was simultaneously on the rolls of five welfare departments—in Boston, New York, Philadelphia, Jersey City and Newark. Sometimes her collection schedule got so hectic she had to fly from New York to Boston and then to Philadelphia. When we had bumped into her outside the bus terminal, she was returning from Newark, where she had just cashed a check for three hundred and twenty-five dollars. It was not all net profit. To certify her local residence, she "rents" an apartment she has never seen in a house which is conveniently next door to a check-cashing establishment. She tele-

phones the landlord to make sure the check has arrived. Then she hops a bus. The landlord passes her
the check, she cashes it and pays him eighty dollars.
The landlord is a Newark cop.

In Boston, where she claimed to have five depen-
dents, Yana managed to skirt this sharing of the wealth
merely by putting up a mailbox with her name on it
inside the entrance of the dilapidated building she had
given as her address. Once, when she was standing in
the foyer, waiting for the check to be delivered, the
postman told her that he knew what she was up to,
that she did not live there, and that he would report
her unless he received a cut. "You do it," she said,
"and I'll have you locked up for rape." That was the
last she heard from the postman.

In between her welfare pickups she was out hustling
—posing as a prostitute around Times Square. She
would entice a man into a hallway to negotiate a price,
murmuring all the things she would do for him, grind-
ing her pelvis and rubbing her belly and breasts against
him, and running her hands up and down his body.
But it is almost unheard of for a gypsy girl to be a
whore, and what her hands were looking for was the
man's wallet. Yana is a very good pickpocket, and
when she had extracted the wallet, she took only some
of the bills, those in the middle, and then slipped the
wallet back into the man's pocket and broke off the
dickering by setting too high a price for her services.
On the rare occasion when a man somehow sensed that
he had been had and cornered her while he counted
his money, she would quickly resort to the traditional
gypsy safety-valve device of dropping the bills on the

ground, accuse him of not being able to hold onto his cash and walk off in a huff.

. An older sister introduced her to the art of picking pockets. "She took me with her one day," Yana said. "This happened in New York when I was around maybe ten, eleven, I think, and we went to Chinatown, and we went into a Chinese laundry where they do shirts and things, and she whispered, 'Go ahead!' I knew her meaning because I was with her many times when she was stealing, but I never tried to steal myself because I was too afraid. This Chinaman in the laundry, he must of been sixty or seventy, an old man, and my sister says to go ahead and put myself on him. 'Try,' she says, 'he ain't got no money anyway, the most he's got is five dollars.' So at first I said no, I didn't want to, I was afraid. And she says, 'There's nothing to it, look how old he is and how big and loose his pants is. Go ahead.' So I put myself towards him and gradually spoke with him, and I was frightened, you know, scared, and all of my hand went into his pocket, right? He grabbed me by the wrist and he started yelling and slapping me, and I was lucky to get out of there." Yana laughed at the memory. "Well, what the hell," she said, "my whole goddamn hand was in his pocket, and that's the way you learn, by your mistakes, and you improve."

There was, she discovered, still more to learn. When she was fourteen and in Los Angeles, she made a fifty-dollar score near "The Strip"—what had become the honky-tonk section of Sunset Boulevard—and instead of immediately returning home and changing her clothes, she had continued wandering around outside the topless bars and nightclubs looking for another victim. Meanwhile the man from whom she had taken the fifty dollars had discovered his loss and reported it along with a description of Yana and what she was wearing, and she was picked up by the police. She was hauled into Los Angeles Juvenile Court and wound up serving nine months in the Ventura School for Girls.

Even though she was now a ringwise veteran, she faced other unexpected moments of peril. Just a few days ago, she said, she had relieved a man of three hundred dollars. "I was generous. I left him six hundred. He must of been a numbers guy or something, carrying money like that." Five minutes later there was a buzz at her door, and the man was at her throat with a screwdriver. "I talked my way out of it," she said. "I made him believe he dropped the money in the hall downstairs, and when we got down there, I said there it is, you creep, leave me alone! If he didn't, I would of kicked him, you know, where it hurts."

Steve looked at her in amazement. "How did he know where you lived?" he said. "You should know better."

"Well, I was just coming out into the street, and he came up to me, and I figured, well, take it while it's there."

I asked Yana if the prostitutes in the area, many of whom were organized, resented her presence, and she replied no, that often one would come up to her and say, "Hey, sister, you got it made. You make the bread and you don't do nothing for it. Teach me how you do it."

"Yana," Steve interjected, "you got to stop stealing."

She turned toward him, hands on hips, and said, "Well, you're the king. You got the medallion and the ring. You're supposed to be leading us out of it." Yana clapped a hand to her head. "What else can I do? I'm a gypsy. It's in our blood."

"Bullshit! It's not your blood. It's the way they brought you up. They brought you up to steal."

"Well, forget about being king and just take me with you."

"I have to find Sonia."

The next day Steve telephoned me. Yana had learned that his sister was in a hospital called Bergen Pines, a few minutes by car past the New Jersey side of the George Washington Bridge. But he had to move fast. His father, using her suicide attempt as an excuse, was going to put Sonia in a sanatorium until she submitted to his will. Steve wanted me to drive him there.

"Why me?" I asked.

"You're lucky," he said. "I get good vibes from you. I'd really appreciate it." He persisted, and somehow succeeded in making me feel guilty if I did not come through, so I agreed.

That afternoon on the way to the hospital, he spoke to me, as he had before, about a singing career he was trying to launch. He said that the furniture-refinishing business which he had started in California—from which he was grossing around fifteen hundred dollars a month, demonstrating to other gypsies that it was possible to get by legitimately—was not enough. That's why his singing career was so important. He had to accomplish something dramatic that would really impress them. He had been appearing on and off in small clubs in the Los Angeles area, and if he ever made it, the money would go to a gypsy foundation to educate gypsy children. It was by not sending their offspring to school and not even letting them play with American children, he said, that gypsies were able to maintain control over them. When gypsy kids reached eleven or twelve, many of them realized what their future would be like, and sneaked off to school on their own.

"Well, that's a twist," I said. "Most kids try to sneak *out* of school."

"Yes," he said, "but it's not so funny. Gypsy kids can't read or write, you know, and they're put in with children half their age, and they take it for a couple of weeks, and they split. After that they're in the life for good." He looked glumly out the car window. "Besides, they know they have the right to steal. It's in the Bible."

"What do you mean, it's in the Bible?"

He then told me a story which I would hear from every gypsy I met. Some of the details varied, but the punchline was always the same. In Steve's version the Roman soldiers crucifying Christ intended to use four nails, but a gypsy stole the fourth nail, the one meant for His heart, and in gratitude Christ, on the cross, declared that gypsies could go on stealing forever.

"You're crazy," I said. "That's not in the Bible."

Like all gypsies, he refused to admit defeat. "What Bible did you read?" he demanded. "Who wrote it?"

From the first I had thought that the mission we were on was ludicrous—that Steve could not just suddenly appear on the scene and spirit his sister out of a hospital when she not only was being held for observation as a would-be suicide but was also a legal minor. And as we approached our destination, I finally voiced my doubts that he would be successful. "Don't worry," he said, "something will happen."

I let him out at the front door and then parked the

car. When I got back to the lobby, he was nowhere to be found. I waited perhaps half an hour before he stepped out of an elevator and said, "I think it's O.K. Come on up. The nurse said she couldn't do nothing, but I got her to call the doctor and I've been talking to her. She's a woman, the doctor, I mean."

On the fifth floor Steve led me around a corner and down a corridor and I saw a girl I knew right away was Sonia, strapped in a wheelchair, hunched over, her face sallow, eyes unfocused. But Steve guided me right past her toward two men standing in front of a door. The door was partially open and I could see a man inside in bed.

One of the men standing in the corridor said, "Well, are you or aren't you?"

"Aren't I what?"

"Are you the guy who wrote *Serpico?*"

The two men turned out to be county detectives guarding a material witness in a forthcoming trial involving organized racketeering. Steve had recognized them as cops when he first came up, and told them about me. I suddenly realized that I was in the middle of another gypsy maneuver. He had intended all along to use me to establish his credentials in trying to get Sonia out of the hospital, and the presence of the cops was just a bonus.

One of the detectives asked me for my autograph, and his partner wanted to know if there was any chance of getting a couple of copies of *Serpico,* and the first one said that it would be nice if I could send a copy to the sheriff as well. They both gave me their cards, and the first detective wrote the sheriff's name on the back of his card.

As the four of us stood there talking, I noticed the floor nurse and the doctor watching us. Steve waited for a few minutes and then stepped over to them, and I heard him say, "I'm telling you, if you don't let her go, she'll try to kill herself again, and you'll be responsible." The doctor walked over to Sonia, who mumbled, "Please, I want to go with my brother," and finally the doctor told the nurse, "All right, let her go."

While the release papers were being filled out and Steve was signing them, it was discovered that the father had taken Sonia's clothes. All she had was what she was wearing, a white hospital gown and cotton slippers. "It doesn't matter," Steve said, "she can go like she is," and borrowed my raincoat to put around her.

I went for the car and picked them up at the front entrance. There is a fairly long approach to the Bergen Pines hospital, and as we were driving away, Steve abruptly pushed Sonia down in the seat and ducked his head. A car sped by us heading for the hospital. "That was Carranza," he said.

The call from the father came later that night. He had obtained the telephone number either from the hospital or from one of the gypsies Steve had called in an effort to locate Sonia. Apparently, however, he had not realized that it was a hotel when the operator answered because the first thing he wanted to know was Steve's address. When Steve refused to tell him, he launched into an incredible, almost crazed string of obscenities. "You motherfucking faggot," he screamed, "I know why you got Sonia, you fucking pimp bastard. You want to make her into your whore." Then he said, "I'm going to find you, sonny boy. My people are going to get you."

Steve hung up on him. Afterward Sonia began to shake uncontrollably, and Steve assured her that everything would be all right, that they would move in the morning. He told me that he had planned to leave the hotel in any event. The hotel management had found out about the puppy he was keeping in his room, and earlier that day an assistant manager had come up and said, "What do you think this is, some kind of kennel? Either the dog goes, or you go."

PART
II

❖

The Boojo

Even if Steve Tene could read, no written gypsy records exist for him to trace his heritage. Most anthropologists believe that gypsies came from Northern India. The best clue they have for this is Romany, which has been classified as belonging to the Indo-Aryan language group. But until relatively recent, and very tentative, efforts to codify it on paper, Romany was only spoken, and whatever ancient catastrophe, man-made or natural, caused the gypsy tribes to emigrate remains unknown.

What *is* certain about gypsies is that they are everywhere in the world today, except possibly in the Far East, and everywhere they have gone they have zealously sustained a racial and cultural entity shielded by a virtually foolproof one-way mirror through which they do all the looking unless they choose otherwise. And it is this determined, now-you-see-us, now-you-don't formula that has helped them to hang together for so long and yet made them a constantly and often brutally harassed minority wherever they have popped up. "Wild outcasts of society," Wordsworth called them.

There is some evidence that they wandered into the Middle East around A.D. 800. Even then they were the object of much hostility, and they kept traveling—in scattered, leap-frogging groups rather than in a single great mass. A few, it is thought, circled around the Mediterranean along the North African coast. More of them left Asia by crossing the Bosporus, and others apparently used the Grecian archipelago, including Crete, as steppingstones to the European mainland. They wandered through the Balkans, many stopping off en route for a more circumscribed nomadic existence, while the rest pushed on. Their first confirmed appearance in Western Europe was in the early fifteenth century. Once within the purview of the Holy Roman Empire, having no organized religion of their own, they quickly ascertained where the power was, and got the name "gypsy," a corruption of Egyptian, as a result of their first major con there—representing themselves as refugee Christians who had been driven from the banks of the Nile by barbaric Moslems.

There were variations on this theme. To ease their way past national borders and to explain their continual movement, a band of gypsies might drop the part the Moslems allegedly played in their exodus from Egypt and say that they had gone to Rome to confess their sins and that the Pope had decreed a seven-year pilgrimage of penance. Never ones to overlook a little swag on the side, they also came complete with "letters" they claimed had been supplied by His Holiness instructing every abbot and bishop they encountered to cross their palms with gold to keep them going. The first gypsies in Paris arrived in 1427 with such letters and, according to an anonymous Parisian counterpart of Samuel Pepys, had the whole city agog. He described the contingent as a raffish lot numbering about a hundred and twenty men, women, and children on foot, led by "twelve penitent lords, a duke, a count, and twelve knights" on horseback. The newcomers, he wrote, had pierced ears and wore silver earrings. The men were very dark-complexioned and had curly hair; the women were ugly and swarthy and had hair as "black as a horse's tail." People turned out in droves to view them not only because of their strange appearance and alien manners but also because the gypsies had brought with them from India the arts of palmistry and fortune-telling. They stirred up trouble between married couples by saying that husbands and wives had been unfaithful to one another, the Parisian's journal continued, and "they emptied the purses of all into their own," although he added that he himself did not personally witness this.

Their awed reception was in any event short-lived. The story of where they came from and what they were doing did not hold up, even in fifteenth-century Paris, their dark looks eventually caused them to be equated with Moors, their exotic customs spawned increasing suspicion and the Bishop of Paris topped things off with an edict that anyone caught having his palm read would be excommunicated. But by then this vanguard of gypsies had already pulled up stakes. A general outline of the initial gypsy migration on the continent seems to wind through southern Europe to France and the Atlantic, followed by a curl north into the Lowlands, back to Germany, into Poland and Lithuania and finally Russia. Splinter groups dropped off along the way, across the channel to England, and into Scandinavia. Around

1470 they were in Spain, just in time for the Inquisition, having crossed the Pyrenees from France, or the Strait of Gibraltar from North Africa, or both.

The trouble is that most of the available literature on gypsies falls into one of two categories. It is written by *gadje*—the Romany plural of *gadjo*—who, seized by wanderlust, joined the gypsies for a time and then penned romantic memoirs of the type later popularized by movies of the 1930s in which the women were wildly passionate and the men basically good-natured knaves ready to break into song at the first screech of a violin, or it has been compiled in apparent scholarly fashion full of footnotes by social scientists who invariably side with the gypsies as a downtrodden race, miserably and unfairly treated by the rest of mankind. In either instance, nobody can get together on what ought to be simple historical fact. Perhaps it is because the subject is gypsies. One seemingly authoritative and sympathetic work, for example, flatly states that during the Spanish Inquisition gypsies were deemed not worth bothering with. Yet another equally authoritative and sympathetic treatise pictures them as being right up there with the Jews and Moors as prime Inquisition targets.

The latter version appears far more likely, since gypsies on the road—women telling fortunes; men occasionally trading horses, working in metal, especially copper, or crafting leather; men, women *and* children stealing anything that was not nailed down—had pretty much the same falling-domino effect wherever they went. At first they were received with fascination, if not friendliness, on the heels of which came a plethora of second thoughts, all bad. In England Henry VIII, taking time out from his quarrels with the Vatican, proclaimed them "Outlandysshe People callynge themselfes Egyptians," and his daughter Elizabeth I ordered all gypsies in Britain expelled forthwith and none, of course, admitted because of their "devilish and naughty Practices." The words may sound quaint, but the punishment for being a gypsy or, for that matter, associating with one, was death. Still, Queen Elizabeth failed in both her deportation and immigration policies, as was the case elsewhere. The gypsies, ever resilient, might lose battle after battle but never the war. The Dutch forbade any Romany crossing of their border and were successful for some thirty years until their fervor slackened, whereupon gypsies promptly reappeared as if nothing had ever happened. The Swiss, for all their fabled thoroughness, tried the same tactics to no avail. In what were then the Italian and Papal States ruthless police pressure was applied against the gypsies; but all it accomplished was to keep them moving, which they would have done anyway. Sometimes gypsies would set up encampments that straddled both sides of a frontier, thus ensuring free passage back and forth should an emergency arise.

Even in nations noted for their openness, gypsies were quickly repressed; in Sweden, as far back as 1637, the gallows was the penalty for a male gypsy caught on the loose, and in Norway anyone apprehended while ferrying in a gypsy had his boat confiscated. In Germany, with typical Teutonic heavy-handedness, city and state governments put up signs showing men being hanged and half-naked women being whipped, along with printed warnings that this would be the fate of all gypsies entering the area. The French were not much more subtle. The police were given free rein, often with murderous results for the men, while many gypsy women and children were confined to workhouses and their heads were shaved.

Not until the nineteenth century did this sort of monstrous behavior against gypsies begin to decrease, although the gypsies remained objects of great legal discrimination. Having given up expulsion as an answer to their unwanted visitors, countries now tried to "cope." In an effort to keep tabs on them, a new approach was to prohibit nomadism, a law that immediately became unworkable as gypsies by the tens of thousands kept right on wandering at will, leaving traditional messages for others in their wake—a piece of cloth fluttering in a tree, a broken twig, lines scratched in the dirt at a fork in the road—that provided basic intelligence about the route a particular caravan was taking, the general mood of the countryside, recent births and deaths, and so on. Next came an attempt, equally fruitless, to erase their Romany identity; the most grandiose try was in the old Austro-Hungarian Empire, which created special settlements where gypsy children would supposedly attend school and church on a regular basis. The British tried a different tack. The first thing to do, it was decided, was to find out exactly what the dimensions of the problem were, and a census was taken. This did not work any better than anything else. Gypsies either could not understand the forms or, through intermediaries, supplied misinformation; some were counted several times as they passed from one region to another, and others did not get counted at all. In France, in 1912, out of official desperation, gypsies were required to carry identity cards that listed, among various items, the length of the bearer's right ear, the distance between his left elbow and left middle finger and the length of his left foot. The complexity alone of these cards was self-defeating, and gypsies rapidly learned which districts rigidly enforced registration and which did not.

Given their circumstances, it was inevitable that the rise of Hitler in Germany would be disastrous for the gypsies. And whatever hope some of them entertained that they would be spared because of their Aryan descent went by the boards when Nazi theoreticians began declaiming, "The Jew and the Gypsy are today far removed from us [racially] because their Asian background is completely different from that of our Nordic forebears." A few German academicians could not bring themselves to dismiss totally the Aryan ancestry of gypsies but noted that they were from the lowest level and had allowed themselves to be mongrelized, living proof of which was their habitual wandering. The Nazis, ignoring history, first tried to get rid of the gypsies through expulsion. Failing in this as everyone before them had, such illustrious butchers of humanity as Heinrich Himmler, Reinhard Heydrich and Adolf Eichmann took over, extermination became the new solution, and gypsies were carted off in wholesale lots to die in such concentration camps as Dachau, Buchenwald, Belsen and Auschwitz. By the end of World War II somewhere between a quarter and a half million gypsies had perished in the gas chambers and other forms of genocide the Hitlerian age had devised.

Still, despite their studied refusal to assimilate, which should have made their destruction all the easier, they survived. And of all those who managed to live through the Nazi holocaust, no race remained more victimized. This was partially due to some gypsy spokesmen who, not content with the actual decimation of their number, wildly exaggerated the death toll, putting it at between three and four million. The figure was so patently absurd that it first tended to put into question the reality of what had happened, which was horrible enough, and then worse yet, once the facts were substantiated, so softened the impact that it barely pricked the conscience of the civilized world.

In postwar France gypsies were still required to carry separate identity cards and report constantly to the police, and everywhere they went they were confronted with municipal signs saying *"Stationnement Interdit aux Nomades,"* which loosely translates into "gypsies forbidden." At one point the government tried to herd gypsies into public-housing projects, compelling them to attend courses in reading and writing and Western hygiene. It seemed like a great idea until officials arrived to find the doors burned as firewood, the plumbing sold as scrap and the gypsies gone. Recently, more diplomatic attempts have been made to get gypsies to settle down by inviting their consultation in new developments and involving them in the construction work. The outcome of such experiments remains in doubt. "Yes, life is better here," a gypsy woman told a reporter, "but we are not happier." In Spain ever since the Inquisition, save for an occasional bullfighter or flamenco singer who has gained recognition on sheer talent, gypsies have stayed a despised people, the "worthless ones," shunted into squalid ghettos, some still dwelling in caves. Isolated by the Pyrenees, subjected endlessly to a fierce brand of tyranny, the gypsies of Spain are different from other gypsies, more trapped than free, many of them unable to speak their ancient tongue, with only a tenuous hold on their heritage. But out of their tortured existence has come the flamenco, which, while indigenous to Spain, has reached its most profound moments in gypsy throats crying out, almost as a primal scream—

> *I'm not from these parts;*
> *I wasn't born here.*
> *The wheel of fortune, spinning, spinning,*
> *Has brought me here.*

In Italy gypsies, perhaps a hundred thousand of them, remain outside the public consciousness, except for a classic caper now and then. One of the most sensational, seemingly full of romance and passion, occurred during World War II when a member of the Italian nobility reported the theft of some jewelry—a five-string pearl necklace, two large emerald rings, a ruby-studded silver bracelet and a diamond tiara, all valued at nearly a million dollars. Eventually, through informants, the police heard that a certain gypsy had committed the theft. He was questioned, finally confessed and then re-enacted the crime step-by-step, including scaling a wall and slipping the latch of a pair of French windows with piano wire. The gypsy, whose name was Guglielmo, was tried and convicted and spent eight years in prison, but other than insisting enigmatically that he had not sold the jewels, he refused to say anything about his crime, and the mystery of what happened to the gems was never resolved. Sixteen years later the Carabinieri received another tip that a beautiful gypsy woman had been seen wearing some of the missing gems. Guglielmo was tracked down and interrogated again, to no avail. "I stole the jewels and paid for the crime," he said in the grand tradition. "Nothing else is important."

In Sweden, meanwhile, immigration is limited to a select fifty families a year, and gypsies there generally stay in one place because of the harsh climate. In Britain, however, they continue to travel in caravans. With the urban sprawl and population growth, favored spots to stop for the night—in a particular meadow by a stream, at the edge of a wooded pond—have become increasingly untenable for the gypsies, who have found themselves being driven off by resentful local authorities. Officials could even overrule a friendly farmer who provided a camping site, and it appeared that traditional English tolerance halted just short of the gypsies. Finally, in 1970, after years of lobbying, citizens who had taken up the gypsy cause got the Caravan Sites Act through Parliament. This required the various localities regularly visited by gypsies to construct sites for them that had water, sewer and electrical facilities. The battle, however, had just begun. Only a fraction of the called-for sites have been completed, gypsies still go where they please and are still hounded, and at each site that has been finished there are cries to outlaw "surplus" gypsies, that is, the number in excess of the quota specified for it. The head of a committee of concerned property owners warned about the hazards they faced if the gypsies were not kept in check. "They can expect their children to be forcibly robbed of clothes and toys, their trees and fences to be systematically pillaged to provide fuel and access for their vehicles onto private lands, and ill-controlled horses to be let loose to graze in playing fields and private gardens," he said in high indignation.

The Russians decided to skip all this capitalist nonsense and deal with the gypsies on solidly rational, Marxist principles. They revealed that gypsies were being supplied with a written version of the Romany language, pointedly noting that this was something gypsies "did not have in other countries." Furthermore, it was added, gypsies were going to have their own national schools; a gypsy press, to say nothing of literature and the theater, was in rapid formation. Next out of Moscow came a smug announcement that gypsies in the Soviet Union had abandoned their footloose habits and were "taking part in building collective farms" and "working as members of cooperatives." One wondered. Did the Russians know something nobody else knew? The answer, a few years later, came in another flash out of Moscow, markedly less effusive this time, which declared that all gypsies who refused to engage in "socially useful labor" were now subject to imprisonment for five years in "corrective" work camps. There was a hurt, testy tone to this decree. The gypsies, it seemed, had insisted on pursuing a "vagrant, parasitic way of life" and, moreover, often committed crimes despite governmental efforts to provide settlements for them. One such settlement might have contained the same gypsies who were in the ill-fated housing project the French had undertaken. The Russian gypsies, in this instance, were conducted to their new quarters just before the onslaught of winter. In the spring, when officials went out to the settlement to suggest perhaps moving on to a collective farm for the summer, all they found were the outer walls and parts of the flooring. Everything else, movable or combustible, was missing, as were the gypsies. For decades the Soviets have had stringent laws on the books outlawing nomadism; at last report they have given up enforcing them.

Only in sections of Yugoslavia and Czechoslovakia, where gypsies have possibly resided the longest and where their life style and ancient occupations as smiths and horse traders are not that dissimilar from those in the surrounding area, have they been able to retain their own identity while participating to a degree in the social and political affairs of the community. Some gypsy-watchers profess to see a new national Romany spirit, an awakening of a collective, organized soul. Among them are an Englishman, Grattan Puxon, who spearheaded the fight to get camping sites for gypsies in Britain, and his colleague Donald Kenrick. A milestone which Puxon and Kenrick cite in this nationalist movement was the crowning in 1937, with much pomp and circumstance, of an "influential" Polish gypsy chieftain named Janusz Kwiek as King of Romany by the Archbishop of Warsaw himself. In his coronation address "Janos I," as he was called, declared that the restoration of a gypsy monarchy had been fulfilled after a lapse of a thousand years. One of the key planks in his future platform was the establishment of an independent gypsy homeland. What Janos I said he had in mind was to ask Mussolini for a grant of territory in Africa between what was then Somalia and recently conquered Ethiopia, a region not especially noted for its gypsy connections. Nonetheless, say Puxon and Kenrick, who knows what would have happened if Hitler's legions had not gone on the march? The trouble is that even acknowledged gypsy experts cannot agree on this or other matters. According to another widely respected authority, Jan Yoors, a gentle, Belgian-born artist now living in New York, who ran away from home at the age of twelve and lived with the gypsies for many years and who has a deep emotional attachment to them, gypsies are essentially unorganizable, either by themselves or by others, and King Janos I, far from being "influential," was considered a pompous joke by most Romany tribesmen.

Some gypsyologists say that there are four basic tribes or "races" of the true *rom*—which is the gypsy word for gypsy—the Lowara, the Tshurara, the Kalderasha and the Muchwaya. But then again, other experts say there are only three; still others at the drop of a hat can single out six or more. Gypsies themselves care not at all about such historical distinctions. It is the social scientists who feel compelled to put them into a great mosaic, but with the gypsies the pieces never fit. And there is a perhaps unbridgeable gap in values between gypsies and the *gadje*. Jan Yoors recalls that during his life with the gypsies he heard about one who was a "millionaire." Finally he met him and found a fellow as bedraggled as any he had ever come across. When Yoors expressed amazement at all the talk he had heard about how rich the man was, a Romany friend patiently explained that the gypsy in question was considered a millionaire not because he actually possessed that much money but because he had spent it.

By the same token, when a gypsy is asked about Romany "races" or "nationalities," he usually speaks of them not as they might once have been but always in the present tense, as Argentinian gypsies, for example, or Mexican, Canadian, French, Spanish, Serbian or Greek. Nomenclature essentially means nothing to a gypsy. Indeed, more often than not, if he is asked what *he* is, he will reply that he is a "Hungarian gypsy" and let it go at that, satisfied that he has instilled in the *gadjo* mind the reassuring and harmless image of a rollicking figure in baggy pants and boots madly sawing away on a fiddle. The gypsy is philosophically content to exist in a perpetual present—"A candle is not made of wax," he says, "but is all flame"—and it is this sense of timelessness that enables him to preserve his identity. It is a rare gypsy who can speak of events even three generations past, yet he is acutely aware of centuries of tradition, of *being* a gypsy. His most intense loyalty goes to his particular clan, and here again names as a rule mean little. Surnames were something required by *gadjo* law, and many of them were acquired at random during migratory travels, first acquired and then changed either for protective coloring or perhaps as a result of a border guard's mispronunciation as a tribe went from country to country. Thus Mihailovich in Russia eventually became Mitchell in America. Sometimes the Romany derivative of a tribal name would be retained. A tribe would take the name of an especially wise or powerful leader. In succeeding tribal generations the original leader's name would simply be pluralized and remain that way until another strong leader rose to take his place and had his name identify the tribe. The Frinkuleschti tribe, which settled in and around New York for a number of years, was named after a gypsy chief called Frinkulo. When a member of the tribe was asked who Frinkulo was, he said, "All I know is he was my father's grandfather or something, and my father told me his father said he was the biggest damn gypsy in Russia."

Steve Tene's clan, the Bimbos, was once called Bimbai, the meaning of which has been lost in time. When gypsies today are asked what "Bimbo" stands for, however, the response is always "tough" or "feared," and since bimbo is an American slang word that was in vogue several decades ago and meant a tough guy, the likelihood is that either Steve's grandfather King Tene Bimbo himself, who was born George Tene, adopted it as the tribe's name, or else a cop, sizing up the old man and having trouble spelling Bimbai, wrote down Bimbo instead, and the grandfather, in line with his terrorist tactics, decided to keep it just so everyone would get the message.

Of the four main gypsy tribes or nationalities, if in fact four is the correct number, at least two—the Kalderasha, which means coppersmiths, and the Muchwaya, from a section of Serbia—are prevalent in the United States. There are some claims that gypsies were here as early as colonial times. But most of them began to filter into the country in the 1860s and 70s. The generally accepted theory of their arrival in the Western Hemisphere is that Spain and Portugal, as part of their deportation programs, shipped them over in the sixteenth and seventeenth centuries to colonies in Latin America, whence they worked their way northward through Central America and Mexico. There are, of course, many exceptions. King Tene's wife, Queen Mary Bimbo, was born in Buenos Aires, Argentina, while he listed his birthplace as New Jersey in enough different documents to lend it a certain credibility, and his people were from Canada, but how they got there none of the Bimbos seems to know.

Since gypsies showed up in the United States, the sole recognizable change in their mode of life has been to travel by car and trailer instead of horse and wagon, and although most of them move about as restlessly as ever, they now go in individual family units rather than the tribal caravans of old. To all intents gypsies have adjusted easily to modern America, yet they still abide by such ancient customs as *marimay,* in which a man *and* his family can be made instantly "unclean," complete social outcasts in the gypsy subculture, by a woman who spitefully lifts her skirt, because of some slight, real or imagined, or some feud, and exposes her genitals to him.

There are endless forms of *marimay,* of varying severity, and gypsies take them all quite seriously. In a house a woman can never pass in front of a man or between two men but only around them. She must always serve a man during dinner from the rear and can never lean across him to pass a dish. When seated, if she is wearing an ordinary dress, she has to cover her legs with a coat or blanket. If a gypsy goes to the bathroom, he must be accompanied by another gypsy who stands outside the door, whether there is a lock or not, to guard against the entry, accidental or on purpose, of a member of the opposite sex. A woman is considered unclean from the waist down, and should a male gypsy happen to touch a woman's skirt and then eat without first washing his hands, he becomes *marimay.* Similarly, if a gypsy, for instance, blows his nose and eats before washing, he or she is *marimay.* Cooking and eating utensils must also be cleaned in a place separate from where humans wash. If a gypsy, however innocently, washes his hands in a sink reserved for pots and pans, he is *marimay.* And conversely, should a forgetful girl rinse off a spoon in a basin used for such bodily ablutions as brushing teeth or gargling and then, even worse, put the spoon in a drawer with other utensils, everything in the drawer must be thrown out immediately. *Marimay,* depending upon its gravity, can only be removed through a complicated process involving the passage of time, possibly the convocation of a gypsy council, the *kris,* to consider the matter, the forgiveness of those present at the moment of transgression and often a visit to a church by the contrite party, who must light candles, pray and swear that whatever the deed, it was done without malice aforethought.

As silly as they seem, most forms of *marimay,* which invariably center on sex and sanitation, date back to the centuries-old caravan life of gypsies and were born of necessity and a desire to preserve some semblance of social order. All the rigmarole about cleaning kitchen utensils and personal hygiene comes from the time when a caravan, camping alongside a river, would designate various parts of it for specific usage. An area the farthest upstream would be reserved for drinking and cooking water; next was a spot for bathing, one for dish water and then, in succession, places to draw water for the horses, to wash clothes generally and finally to scrub the clothes of menstruating women. Sexual promiscuity in such close quarters was an ever-present danger, and the strictures concerning women were designed to draw a proscribed circle around them down to the smallest detail of everyday life; as for the *marimay* in lifting their skirts, it was meant to give them added protection if they were attacked, since, then as now, the worst punishment a gypsy can possibly imagine is to be ostracized by his tribe.

There are other taboos as well. When a gypsy mother happens to have twins, one will be immediately sold to another family because of the bad luck that will befall her should she keep them both. If this sounds irrational about a people who prey for profit on the superstitions of others, the only thing really contradictory about gypsies would be a lack of contradiction. While they project a romantic, carefree existence, it is in fact frequently cruel, and discipline is rigidly enforced. On one hand, gypsies claim with reason that they are a persecuted people; on the other, they remain steadfastly apart from the rest of the community and are violently prejudiced themselves, notably against blacks. Male dominance is absolute, yet women do practically all the work and earn most of the money. Gypsies profess envy of the world of the *gadjo*, but they are secretly contemptuous of it.

On the latter count, they would appear to have every right to their opinion. Not only do they ignore the constraints, legal and otherwise, that bind ordinary citizens, but they get away with it. And after untold years, one of the oldest of the gypsy swindles, the *boojo* (also pronounced, incorrectly, *boujour*) continues to work on credulous *gadje* as if everyone were preserved in amber; indeed, with the advent of movies and books like *The Exorcist* and other forms of revival that the devil has been experiencing recently, business is better than ever.

A *boojo* is as formalized in structure as a Greek

tragedy. It usually begins in a gypsy fortune-telling joint, the *ofisa*. Anyone who goes into an *ofisa*, however, gets very little of the future for the two or five dollars that is automatically demanded nowadays. What the *boojo* woman is looking for is that one person in a hundred, in five hundred, whom she can exploit. She can afford to be patient. Police files are dotted with individual scores in the thousands of dollars, and the evidence suggests that the vast majority of cases go unreported because the victim is too ashamed or, incredibly enough, remains a believer. One distraught lady finally went to the police after she had been taken for thirty-two thousand dollars, not to complain that she had been bilked out of her money but that the curse she had paid to have removed was still hanging over her head.

As soon as she can, the *boojo* woman tries to ferret out the reason that prompted a potential victim to enter her establishment. "I see you're a good person," she will say perhaps. "You're honest and you smile in your face, but deep inside you don't smile the way you should. Maybe you toss and turn in your bed at night. Something's troubling you, that's for sure." Few people, as she is well aware, are going to argue with her thus far. The *boojo* woman sighs with the sigh of one who has seen it all and knows all, and then she will say, "Listen to me. Make two wishes. Keep one to yourself and tell me the other. But don't wish for possessions because possessions are not important. It's your health and happiness that count."

The hope is that the articulated wish involves a personal crisis of some kind, preferably a terminally ill parent, a retarded child, a tormenting marital problem, an investment gone sour. Surrounded by all the trappings of a seer—a darkened room, candles, some strategically hung tapestries, pictures of the Holy Family on the wall, an astrology chart, tarot cards, books on witchcraft—the *boojo* woman listens sympathetically, and at last, when the proper psychological moment has arrived, she suggests that the misfortune under discussion may have been brought about by cursed money that the victim has put away, possibly in a savings account. It doesn't matter, she says, if the original cash is gone; that's the problem with a curse, it just jumps to whatever new money comes into hand. In any event a test must be made, and she tells the victim to return the next day with a designated number of bills, usually nine, in different denominations. If the money is not tainted, other avenues will be explored. If it is, she will at once do her best to remove the curse.

The only test, of course, is to see if the victim follows the instructions, since the money always turns out to be cursed. There are several methods the *boojo* woman employs to prove this. One of the old standbys, no longer in much use, was to tell the victim to bring a live chicken along with the money. The *boojo* woman would cradle the chicken, surreptitiously fingering a key vein just below its neck, and reach for a bill. She would wave the bill in a circle around the chicken, invoking various arcane spirits, and then touch the bird here and there with it. Her fingers, meanwhile, would press down on the vein; there would be an abbreviated squawk or a brief flurry of feathers before she and the victim were left with one mysteriously but dramatically dead chicken. Because of the difficulty involved in acquiring a live chicken these days, especially in cities, the trick has been largely abandoned. It was given up reluctantly, however, since even in times past it required considerable effort on the victim's part to get and lug a cackling chicken to an *ofisa,* and if the assignment was carried out, the *boojo* woman had a pretty good idea of the potential influence she could exert over her target.

Another old device, the "boiling water" routine, remains in favor. The *boojo* woman takes the bills and wraps them with a rubber band around a glass of water about three-quarters full, and over the top of the glass she stretches a piece of cloth held tight by a second rubber band. The presence of a curse will be revealed, she explains, if the water boils without benefit of fire. So saying, she quickly turns over the glass onto a plate, and the displaced air inside the glass impressively bubbles up on cue. Still another tried-and-true gimmick is to have the victim bring an egg together with the cash. The *boojo* woman breaks the egg in a plate and, with expert sleight-of-hand, places a tiny, carved devil's head or a pinch of hair in the yolk, a rather awesome sight. A new wrinkle is to take a dollar from the nervous victim, carefully fold it and pretend to drop it into a bowl of water. But the *boojo* woman has switched the bill for another one, similarly folded, containing dye. Afterward both she and the victim silently contemplate the water as it slowly turns blood-red.

The *boojo* woman then hastily hands back the money as if fearful of being contaminated herself. Now it is up to the victim to ask what must be done. Every *boojo* woman plays it by ear, relying upon instinct and experience to decide what is possible or probable. She may sense that someone who has wandered into her *ofisa* needs further convincing before succumbing to her control. So she will ask the victim for a five-dollar bill, pretending to slip it inside a folded piece of cloth but actually substituting a ten-dollar bill of her own. She sews up the cloth, generally a handkerchief, and prays for the victim's future good fortune, asking that his money be doubled as proof of this. Then she gives the handkerchief to the victim and instructs him to sleep with it under his pillow for three nights before opening it. There is case after case in police files of victims sucked in by this device. They go home, wait the three days and then look inside the handkerchief. They find the bill magically doubled and rush back to the *boojo* woman with all the available cash they have, only to find that the next time around the handkerchief contains nothing but sheaves of paper.

Sometimes, if a victim appears to have limited funds, the *boojo* woman may settle for the purchase of "holy" candles—costing twenty-five, fifty, or a hundred dollars—which must be lit while she prays for the removal of a curse. Or she may name a sum necessary to break the evil spell that she knows the victim can't come up with all at once, but in an apparent burst of generosity she offers to go to her "church" to borrow the money, which can be repaid on a weekly basis. Nothing fazes her. If a person on the installment plan complains of continuing bad luck, she will reply that this is because the victim has privately doubted her power, that as a result everything is going to be twice as difficult to fix, and will forthwith double each payment.

There are, indeed, occasions when a *boojo* woman has to do practically nothing to make a big score. In

Boston a widow walked into an *ofisa* operated by a member of the Bimbo clan and revealed that her recently deceased husband had left a twenty-thousand-dollar insurance policy, half of which was for her and half for their only son. The problem was that the son was going out with a trashy girl, not worth a minute of her son's time, who was just after his share of the inheritance. The widow, according to her eventual complaint to the police, said that she herself did not care about the money but needed advice on how to break up her son's romance. The *boojo* woman considered the problem briefly and said that an enemy of the dead husband had put a curse on him and the curse had passed on to the insurance money. The sole solution was for the widow to bury the cash in the husband's grave.

"You mean I have to go into the cemetery with a shovel?" the widow asked.

"Yes, dear, and you got to do it at midnight," the *boojo* woman said. "At the stroke of twelve, you know what I mean? You want to take away the curse and save your son, this is what you must do. Usually you got to be naked too."

"Oh, my God," the widow recalls saying, "I couldn't do anything like that."

The *boojo* woman solemnly replied that while it was a hard thing to ask of anybody, in this instance she would act as the widow's surrogate, and the grateful widow gave her the money.

It is the thought of getting somebody to part with a substantial amount of cash that so warms a *boojo* woman's heart. A number of prayerful consultations are generally required to ascertain how much has been tucked away by a victim in a savings account or shoe-box. A good *boojo* woman doesn't mind the time; she applies to her craft all the perseverance of a surfcaster waiting for a passing striped bass to hook itself on his line. And along the way, just to be on the safe side, the sucker is made to perform some act of physical obei-sance, such as kneeling and kissing the *boojo* woman's foot. This is partially to reinforce psychological con-trol, but it is also to ensure that a cop has not come into the premises, since it is an article of faith among gypsies that no police officer, however expert an un-dercover operative he or she may be, will submit to an indignity like that.

Once the idea has been instilled in a victim that cursed money is at the root of his or her problem, the main thing is to get the victim to bring the cash to the *ofisa*. While both men and women have been duped over and over again, the *boojo* swindle has enjoyed special success with women, particularly those who are middle-aged or older, and law-enforcement officials have secretly taped a session in an *ofisa* where a *boojo* was approaching its final stage. The victim was a wom-an in her early fifties who was convinced that "some-thing" was growing inside her body.

"It's just like I thought," the *boojo* woman said. "The money you got in that bank has got a curse on it, and that's why you got that thing in you. You got to go to that bank and draw the money out, and I got to hold it and get in connection with the right spirits and ask them to throw the curse off."

"But it's all the money I have. What will happen if I don't?"

"Listen, dear," the *boojo* woman said, "it don't make

no difference to me what you do. I'm not getting anything out of this. I got nothing to lose. I'm doing my part, the spirits are using me. You do your part, and the spirits will throw the curse off the money, and that thing you got growing inside of you will go away. You don't do your part, I'm not responsible for what happens, you know. I got nothing growing inside of *me*. I'm just trying to help you."

The *boojo* woman vividly described what would happen to the victim if the "thing" inside her continued to grow, how her hair and teeth would fall out, how her body would erupt in open sores, how her blood would begin to congeal and breathing would become increasingly difficult, and how her heart would pound erratically, and how the pain would start, slowly at first, then faster and faster until she couldn't stand it and would beg to die, but death would not come quickly, death would be a lingering, drawn-out affair, agonizing to the last second.

"Do I have to take out all the money I have?" the victim asked.

"Every cent," the *boojo* woman said. "You don't draw every cent, it isn't worth anything, all this. The curse just stays with the money you left in there, see?" To make things more convenient, the *boojo* woman advised her victim to withdraw the money in large-denomination bills—"After all," she said, "you don't want to lose some of it"—and also warned her to keep the reason for the withdrawal "confidential" should someone inquire about it. "Tell them you're making an investment," the *boojo* woman said. "Whose business is it anyway?"

When the money has been brought to the *ofisa,* an

interplay of fast hands and fast talk begins. A key
prop is a handkerchief in which the money is placed.
Either fake money is switched for the real cash, which
disappears inside the *boojo* woman's blouse or one of
the voluminous pockets in her skirt, and the handkerchief is sewn up while the victim watches; or else the
handkerchief is sewn up with the real money still in it
and, at an appropriate moment, is switched with another handkerchief that holds fake money or sheaves of
paper. All of this is accompanied by much hand
movement, rending of garments, even rolling about on
the floor, and incantations of a steadily increasing deci-
bel count. Often, as the *boojo* woman is thrashing
around, she invites the victim to join her in prayer,
to kneel down, close her eyes and hold her hand, saying,
"Pray with me, dear, this is a powerful curse and we
need all the help we can get. Pray in your own words,
you know what I mean, so we get the right answer."
It is then, in all the confusion and near-hysterical mum-
bo jumbo, that the *boojo* woman, if she has settled on
the technique of switching handkerchiefs, one containing the real money and the other the fake, actually
makes the switch. She reaches into a pocket in her skirt
and feels for several bundles she has already prepared
and selects the one that most closely matches the size
of the handkerchief with the real money in it.

When the curse has been exorcised, the victim is
cautioned not to open the handkerchief for six months
or a year, or the curse will come back, causing the
money inside to turn into what in fact it now is. The
length of time before the handkerchief can be opened
often depends on how many other dupes the *boojo*
woman has in the offing, since an *ofisa* can be disman-

tled and the *boojo* woman on her way out of town within half an hour. There is also another method of winding things up. If a *boojo* woman decides that she is in absolute command of the situation, her domination over the victim unquestioned, she will declare that despite everything she has tried, the curse is too strong; the money in the handkerchief must be burned, and she makes the victim do it on the spot. This "burn-up," as the gypsies call it, has the advantage of practically eliminating the possibility of the switch ever being discovered and also allows the *boojo* woman to remain in contact with the victim for more advice—and more money. The known record in the United States for keeping someone on the hook is sixteen years, and according to the New York Police Department, the biggest score on record in a *boojo* swindle, which happened to include a burn-up, was $118,273. Although it riles members of the Bimbo tribe, who like to think that they are pre-eminent in the *boojo* and who hint darkly, and quite probably correctly, that there have been larger, unreported scores, the *boojo* woman in this case was from another gypsy clan, the Adamses. Her name was Volga Adams, also known as Mary Valda, Olga Morgan, Valda Johnson, Olga Adams, Olga Williams and Mary Adamo or Adams.

The victim was Mrs. Frances Friedman. At the time, Mrs. Friedman was forty-nine and living in New York. She was a small, shapely, auburn-haired woman with a slightly hesitant, uncertain manner, and she had been a widow for nearly eight years. Although Mrs. Friedman had two daughters, one of whom was married and had a daughter of her own, she was, by her own admission, "very lonely" and wanted to meet a man, prefer-

ably a younger man. "My oldest daughter and her husband had lived with me," she would explain later.
"Their child had been born in my house. They had
left and moved out of town." Her other daughter, she
said, had finished college but wanted to live by herself. "I felt almost not needed, and that's a bad thing
for a woman."

Around 6 P.M. on September 12, 1956, as she recalled, Mrs. Friedman, accompanied by her sister, left
a doctor's office in the East Seventies in Manhattan and
started walking up Madison Avenue. At 994 Madison
Avenue they passed a gypsy storefront. Mrs. Friedman
had not been feeling well, troubled by a number of
vague ailments she could not really put her finger on.
Other things were also bothering her. Her little granddaughter had a running, open sore that would not go
away, and this made her brood again about a severe
eczema condition one of her daughters had been
afflicted with since birth. And while she wanted des-
perately to meet a man, she could never find one who
measured up to "my husband's qualities," and even
more frustrating and perplexing, she found herself acting "cold" toward men in general.

So on impulse, still with her sister, she went into the
storefront to buy a horoscope. She was just in that
frame of mind, she would testify, and although she had
purchased horoscopes on occasion before, it was the
first time she had ever been in a gypsy emporium. A
gypsy woman, whom Mrs. Friedman later identified as
Volga Adams but whom throughout their relationship
she knew only as "Lillian" or "Lil," told the sisters
that she did not have any horoscopes for sale and
offered to tell their fortunes instead. The sisters had

their fortunes told separately. "Lillian" gave Mrs. Friedman's sister short shrift. But when her turn came to step into a curtained-off section in the rear of the *ofisa,* Mrs. Friedman apparently expressed enough anxiety to arouse "Lillian's" interest, and she was told to return the next morning, that the gypsy had "something important" to tell her. "I don't remember anything especially," Mrs. Friedman said in trying to reconstruct the scene. "Except that what she told me seemed to bring out important things that made me have confidence in her, and I felt she had understanding and sympathy."

When Mrs. Friedman went back to the *ofisa* the following morning, she revealed everything that had been tormenting her, her unfathomable peakedness, her granddaughter's open sore, her daughter's skin condition, her inability to meet the right man. "Lillian" listened and hazarded an opinion that confirmed Mrs. Friedman's worst suspicions about herself, that she was possessed by an "evil" that had been causing all the trouble. In any event, "Lillian" told her, a test would have to be made to "hatch out the evil," and she instructed Mrs. Friedman to take an egg, wrap it in one of her husband's old handkerchiefs, put it overnight in her left shoe and then bring the egg to the *ofisa* for inspection within twenty-four hours. Mrs. Friedman did as she was directed, and gasped in horror as she watched "Lillian" crack the egg she thought she had brought, only to see in place of the yolk a tiny devil's head, greenish-yellow in color, complete with minuscule horns, eyebrows and a little black goatee. Even on the witness stand Mrs. Friedman, when she recalled the moment, became visibly shaken.

"Lillian" had made it clear that she was so concerned about Mrs. Friedman's predicament that she was not going to charge anything for her consultations. And after the episode with the devil's head, she took a dollar bill and with a flourish and some incantations ripped it in half, blessed the torn halves with a small crucifix and seemingly wrapped them in a handkerchief which she pinned inside Mrs. Friedman's brassiere. Mrs. Friedman was ordered to leave the handkerchief untouched in the brassiere for three days and then return with it. "Don't take it off," she was warned. "If the dollar is whole again on the next visit, God is with us."

When Mrs. Friedman went into the *ofisa* for the fourth time and "Lillian" unfolded the handkerchief, the bill was of course miraculously in one piece again. By now "Lillian" could do no wrong in Mrs. Friedman's eyes, and she listened avidly as the significance of the torn bill that "God made whole" was explained. It meant, "Lillian" said, that all of the evil in Mrs. Friedman had been caused by cursed money, and she offered to cleanse it. Mrs. Friedman readily revealed her financial situation. As it happened, she was relatively well off. Among other things, her late husband had left her a one-third interest in a dress company which was subsequently sold. Her part of the proceeds were invested in government bonds with a maturity value of $87,500. She also had five savings accounts of nine thousand dollars, five thousand, seventy-five hundred, sixty-seven hundred and two thousand, as well as a sixth account she used for living expenses. "Lillian" told her to withdraw the money from all the accounts except the one she used for expenses—the problem, she said, was just with the money "sitting there"—and to put the cash in her safe deposit box, making sure to stack the bills in the form of a cross. Once again Mrs. Friedman did as she was instructed.

She continued to have consultations with "Lillian" at the original *ofisa* and then in another one farther uptown at 1350 Madison Avenue. Shortly after Mrs. Friedman put the cash in the safe deposit box, "Lillian" got an unexpected bonus. The open sore on Mrs. Friedman's granddaughter suddenly cleared up. In gratitude she gave "Lillian" some lingerie, and "Lillian" in turn presented her with a good-luck brooch that she claimed had been handed down from generation to generation in her tribe. But when nothing else in Mrs. Friedman's life seemed to improve, "Lillian" said that it must be the money invested in the bonds, that they must be dispensed with at once and the money secreted in the safe deposit box in the form of another cross. Double crosses, "Lillian" suggested, might do the trick. Mrs. Friedman cashed the bonds at their then current worth—$78,073—but had to rent another deposit box to house all the cash. The number of the first box was 1233 and the new one was 3123, and Mrs. Friedman would recall that she thought the fact they were the same numbers, although in a different sequence, boded well.

Still, Mrs. Friedman's daughter went on suffering from eczema, and the man of her dreams had yet to appear. "Lillian" advised her that sterner measures were required, and she was told to bring all the cash to the *ofisa,* along with a live chicken, for a final exorcism.

Mrs. Friedman, according to her testimony, never questioned the money but balked at the chicken, and "Lillian" said that she would supply one herself.

On October 17 or 18, she could not remember which, Mrs. Friedman arrived at the *ofisa* with the cash. In the rear she noted two new items—a chicken running around and a large ash can. She gave the money to "Lillian," who put it in a bag, and that was the last Mrs. Friedman ever saw of it. "Lillian" grabbed the chicken, holding it firmly, and stuck its head inside the bag. The chicken died immediately, and "Lillian" flung it at the stunned woman's feet, screaming that the cursed money had killed the chicken and that there was no alternative except to burn it. With that Mrs. Friedman saw her toss the bag, supposedly containing $108,273, into the ash can. Moments later smoke began pouring out of it. Another gypsy appeared, put a stick into the ash can and began stirring vigorously. Smoke was billowing all through the *ofisa*, and "Lillian," still screaming that she had to burn the money to end the evil, started opening windows.

Mrs. Friedman remained speechless, but the money-burning had not come as a total surprise; "Lillian" had mentioned the possibility of it happening. "The money was the cause of evil," Mrs. Friedman said. "I had hoped against hope until the very day I brought it there that it wouldn't have to be burned. Maybe it was a foolish hope, but I did hope so." Mrs. Friedman tried to explain. "I believed in the ability of 'Lil' to help me with my—with what was termed evil in me and which meant that I was hurting my grandchild, my daughter, with what they had, and also it meant the coldness I felt toward men. And that is why I gave it to her. The money was part of the evil. . . ."

After things had quieted down in the *ofisa*, "Lillian" suggested to Mrs. Friedman that she get away from it all and go to the mountains for "some fresh air" and said she herself was going away for a while but naturally would pray for Mrs. Friedman. Mrs. Friedman took her advice and spent about two weeks at Grossinger's, a well-known resort in the Catskills north of New York City. Upon her return to her apartment on Manhattan's Upper West Side, Mrs. Friedman testified, she received several phone calls from "Lillian," including one from Tucson, Arizona, in mid-December during which "Lillian" said that she was sending Mrs. Friedman a pocketbook as a Christmas gift. Mrs. Friedman received the pocketbook but heard nothing more from the *boojo* woman until July 1957, when she phoned to say she was returning to New York. The two women met in Central Park, and when "Lillian" asked her how she was, Mrs. Friedman replied that she still felt the same. "Lillian" then explained that the original amount of money Mrs. Friedman had given her was not "numerically correct" and that was why she was having such difficulty in helping her. The evil still lurked in her because of money, but another ten thousand dollars ought to resolve everything. "Lillian" assured Mrs. Friedman that burning the cash would not be necessary this time; she would pray over it to get rid of the curse.

On August 6, 1957, Mrs. Friedman brought the additional ten thousand to a West Side hotel "Lillian" was staying in, the Park Plaza. Throughout 1958 and the first half of 1959, "Lillian" called Mrs. Friedman from various parts of the country and they would have long, soulful conversations about Mrs. Friedman's condition. On April 15, 1959, "Lillian" telephoned from Los Angeles, and now she said that there was nothing left to do except destroy the ten thousand, which she presumably had been carting around with her. For the first time Mrs. Friedman objected. She was running low on funds, she said, and she needed the money, cursed or not. "Lillian" tried to argue her out of this, but when Mrs. Friedman became increasingly stubborn, "Lillian" said that she would return at least part of the money when she came to New York in September. The September visit never materialized. Instead Mrs. Friedman received another call from "Lillian," who said that she was in Birmingham, Alabama, and that she wanted Mrs. Friedman to meet her there. Mrs. Friedman replied that this was too far for her to go. "Lillian" then suggested Washington as a compromise, but Mrs. Friedman insisted upon New York, and "Lillian" refused.

At long last Mrs. Friedman faced up to the dreadful truth that had been gnawing at her for months. Indeed, when she handed over the final ten thousand dollars, she had written down the serial numbers of the bills, although this was to be of little help. Not only did Mrs. Friedman have to confront the fact that she had been had but also the public humiliation which she knew she would have to endure—the kind of shame a *boojo* woman counts on to keep her victims quiet.

On September 9, 1959, Mrs. Friedman went to her local precinct station and wound up in the presence of Detective Allen Gore, who was then the police department's gypsy specialist. For Al Gore, Mrs. Friedman solved a mystery that had been rankling him for three years. All through the fall of 1956 Gore had picked up rumors about a *boojo* woman who was making a big score in New York, but he had been unable to pin down the details until Mrs. Friedman sat by his desk. Gore listened to her story and showed her about a hundred mug shots of *boojo* women before Mrs. Friedman recognized "Lillian," a new alias Gore could now add to the others for Volga Adams, aged forty-two, who had been arrested and fined on larceny and fortune-telling charges three times in New York City, once in Cedar Rapids, Iowa, and once in Salinas, California, and who had been arrested but had beaten similar charges in Fresno, California, again in New York, and in Worcester, Massachusetts, among other places. On September 23, Volga Adams became officially sought by the New York Police Department for swindling Mrs. Friedman out of $118,273, and Gore, with the help of the FBI, located her where she had last called Mrs. Friedman from, in Birmingham. Volga Adams fought extradition on the grounds that she was not in New York City when the alleged swindle took place, and Gore and Mrs. Friedman journeyed to Alabama to testify. The proceedings appeared to be going smoothly until Volga Adams suddenly switched to new lawyers who, as the Manhattan district attorney's office learned, supposedly had high political contacts in the state, and her extradition was denied.

That seemed to end the matter, but because of the amount of money involved, along with some jeering phone calls from Birmingham placed by George Adams, Volga's husband, to the effect that Gore would never "get" his wife, the detective continued to keep tabs on Volga Adams. And his tenacity paid off early in the spring of 1961, when he got a tip that she had been spotted in the Miami area. She was arrested, and a new round of extradition hearings was held. They dragged on for more than five months, during which time Volga Adams remained in custody. Gore and Mrs. Friedman went to Florida to testify again, and the *boojo* woman's defense was the same as in Alabama. She claimed that she had not been in New York when the crimes she was accused of occurred. A gypsy woman who identified herself as Lillian Lee of Roanoke, Virginia, swore she was the occupant of the *ofisa* at 994 Madison Avenue that Mrs. Friedman first entered in September 1956 and that "Mary" Adams, as Volga was also known, had never been there. She further testified that she had told Mrs. Friedman's fortune for fifteen dollars and never saw her again. Two other gypsy women, Catherine Uwanowich, who said she was from Tarboro, North Carolina, and Duda Adams, of Chicago, claimed that they were in the second *ofisa* at 1350 Madison Avenue and that "Volga" had never been on the premises. Both Catherine Uwanowich and Duda Adams acknowledged giving a few "readings" to Mrs. Friedman, but, as Duda Adams described them, "It wasn't no personal type readings or anything. She used to come in, and she'd probably give us five or ten or fifteen dollars to read for her. She said she was lonely and she wants to find a man, and if she would ever find a man."

There was a new revelation at the Florida extradition hearings. Volga's husband George had been the lessee for both *ofisas* Mrs. Friedman had visited, the one at 994 Madison Avenue having been rented by him for the purpose of retailing "Pan American Gifts, Novelties and Pottery." The second *ofisa,* he volunteered, was "across the street from the Police Academy," as though this somehow established its legitimacy. What he was talking about was an armory, since torn down, in which the city's mounted police troop quartered its horses. George Adams swore that at the time of the alleged burning of the money in October 1956 he and his wife were in Arkansas and that in August 1957, when Mrs. Friedman said she had forked over ten thousand dollars more, they were residing in Mississippi. The fact that his name appeared on the leases, Adams declared, meant nothing, since he earned his living as a "rental agent" for gypsies. "I rent stores and various tearooms for various gypsies that hasn't got the proper background to meet qualifications to rent in New York City," he said. "What I mean by qualifications is references."

Extradition may have been denied in Alabama but it was allowed in Florida, and she was taken to New York for trial. After several postponements, it got under way on February 23, 1962.

The prosecutor was a gung-ho assistant district attorney, Burton Roberts, who at one point had a professional magician standing by in court to duplicate all the tricks Mrs. Friedman had found so miraculous. And in preparation for the devil's-head-in-the-egg gimmick, as allegedly practiced by Volga Adams, Detective Gore drew the assignment of pinpricking a dozen eggs and blowing the yolks out of them, a chore that left him somewhat queasy. "I hit one double yolk," he told reporters, "and I thought I'd die."

But the defense, concerned about the effect that an

actual demonstration might have on the jury, conceded
that these "tricks," as a defense lawyer sarcastically put
it, were not of supernatural origin, so Roberts was
forced to describe rather than dramatically show how
sleight-of-hand was responsible for the devil's head
once the egg had been prepared, how sleight-of-hand
was the way a torn dollar bill appeared to be put together again, how a chicken could be killed by exerting
pressure on its heart or over a vein in its neck, how
sleight-of-hand was again involved in switching the bag
with the money in it and dropping another one with
sheaves of paper into the fire in the ash can or, for
that matter, how the bag with the money could actually
have been dropped into the can and smoke simulated
from a nonexistent fire by mixing hydrochloric acid
with ammonia. The defense contended, as always, that
while Mrs. Friedman might have been bilked by a gypsy, Volga was not the one who did it. Volga Adams,
one of her lawyers argued, was "just a petty gypsy, a
fortune-teller, not in the class of someone who would
steal over a hundred thousand dollars." Since the time
Mrs. Friedman and her sister had first visited the *ofisa,*
Volga, or "Lillian," had lost considerable weight, and
the sister was unable to make a positive identification.
Another defense attorney pushed Mrs. Friedman on her
mental state and asked if she had ever suffered a head
injury, and throughout the trial spectators in the court-
room nudged one another, and some were heard to say,
"How could she have given away all that money? How
could she fall for something like that?"

Mrs. Friedman, of course, was the least able to provide what is called a reasonable explanation, and the

trial terminated in a hung jury. Assistant district attorney Roberts was determined to try the case again, but just before it was to begin, a year later, defense attorneys for Volga Adams announced that in return for dropping all other counts in the indictment, she would plead guilty to grand larceny in the second degree involving the ten thousand dollars Mrs. Friedman had given her at the Hotel Park Plaza in 1957. Burton Roberts, representing the people, said that the twenty-one months Volga Adams had already spent in custody, first in Florida for the extradition hearings and then in New York, would be acceptable as sufficient punishment.

Volga Adams remained defiant to the end. When the presiding judge asked if she was freely willing to plead guilty to the reduced charge and understood its meaning, she snapped, "Yes, I stole the ten thousand dollars from Frances Friedman. Satisfied?"

Volga had a special word for Roberts. She said that she was putting a "gypsy curse" on him, that he would never marry and would never have children. Whereupon Roberts, who is renowned for his theatrical air, waved his arms around a good deal and retorted that he was putting a "Jewish curse" on her. Since then Roberts, who is now a New York State Supreme Court Justice, has been the butt of many jokes. He is still a bachelor and has no offspring, "at least as far as we know," one of his waggish friends says.

The cash in the Frances Friedman case was never recovered, although a gypsy informant told Detective Gore that Volga Adams once boasted to him in Florida that she had made a big score from a woman in New

York for curing a child. According to the informant, Volga said that she had "made a lot of money and spent over fifty thousand of it for property in California."

Detective Eddie Coyne succeeded Gore as the New York Police Department's gypsy specialist about a year after the Friedman case was concluded. He is one of a long line of gypsy experts the department has had, all of whom have been attached to the pickpocket and confidence squad. Coyne, a square-jawed Irishman, now forty-two, still remembers the day his commanding officer called him and said that he had an assignment for him but that Coyne did not have to accept it unless he wanted to. The assignment was covering gypsy activity in the city, and Coyne's superior warned that it would be a difficult one in which he could expect to be continually accused of shakedowns, taking bribes, consorting carnally with underage females and "God knows what else" a gypsy might think of.

Coyne immediately took the job. He is the kind of cop who likes a challenge and is also one who enjoys working out in the street, which was a major part of his new duty. But he quickly learned how tricky it could be. When he first started surveying *ofisas* in the city, he went into one where the husband of the resident *boojo* woman engaged him in a lengthy conversation, obviously trying to work his way into Coyne's good graces. Then the gypsy asked Coyne if he knew about a new *ofisa* that had just opened up several blocks away. Coyne replied that he did not, thanked the gypsy for the information and said he would look the place over. When Coyne dropped by the second *ofisa* the next day, he found that the gypsy husband there was not at all surprised to see him, was very much on edge and quite relieved as he departed. This kind of thing happened a few more times before Coyne discovered that he was being used as a pawn in a shakedown. The first gypsy, after telling Coyne about a new *ofisa,* would run to the second gypsy and warn him that a cop who was "my man" was coming soon but that things could be fixed for a price. The payoff from the second gypsy to the first was usually in two installments. The initial payment was made on the spot, and the next one was made when Coyne, who was only on an inspection tour, left without doing anything.

Coyne considers the Bimbos the worst of all the gypsy tribes. Generally when he has to go into an *ofisa* for one reason or another, he is greeted at least with civility, and most gypsies, if they think they are in some kind of trouble, will attempt to con their way past him with great protestations of injured innocence. But the Bimbos, he says, are on him in a flash, screaming that they know he is "on the take," that he has been fooling around with their women and they are not going to stand still for this any more, that they will go to the mayor, the governor, the Supreme Court! He also knows that a member of the Bimbo tribe once pulled a pistol on a Massachusetts state trooper and tried to gun him down.

But while the Bimbos are bad enough, members of the Adams tribe give them a good run for rapaciousness, and one of Coyne's biggest headaches in recent times was caused by some Adamses. In 1970 law-enforcement agencies all over the country began receiving communications with an impressive letterhead that read "National Gypsy Crime Investigators, Inc." and bore a Baton Rouge, Louisiana, postal box number. Those that were addressed to police and prosecutors in New York City and State began, "The undersigned is a corporation organized under the laws of the State of Louisiana for the purpose of promoting the welfare of gypsies throughout the United States and to aid law enforcement officials not only with regard to charges made against gypsies but to aid such law enforcement agencies in eliminating fake and illegal racket operations such as palmists, spiritual advisors and mediums which bilk the public out of money."

The letter went on to say that the organization was anxious to improve the lot of gypsies, to promote educational facilities for them and to help them adjust to the laws of the various localities they settled in. "We have extended our services beyond Louisiana," the letter stated, "and have been authorized to perform these services in the State of Georgia. We are presently in the process of setting up an office in the State of New York and have applied to the Secretary of State for designation of our membership corporation under the General Corporation Law."

Getting down to cases, the letter then announced, "We would appreciate it if you would consider us in your investigations and use our assistance in any unlawful activity that may carry the guise of 'gypsy' since it is our purpose to help remove this stigma from our people." It concluded on an upbeat note: "We look forward to hearing from you and trust ours can be a pleasant, fruitful and cooperative association."

There were other, more emotional communications. "We're tired of the image the word 'gypsy' projects," one said. "We have families, people working in respect-

THE BIMBO GYPSIES

King Tene Bimbo in 1924, when he had
achieved supremacy among Chicago gypsies.

King Tene's son Carranza, Steve's father, in 1939.

Pete Bimbo (*left*) **and an unidentified Bimbo woman**
(*center, standing*) **with Pete's father and mother, King Tene
and Queen Mary, in 1930. The picture was taken shortly
after the bloody riot near Methuen, Massachusetts, in which
they all played a part. The inset photo is of another of
King Tene's children, Rose Bimbo, a flamboyant young
woman who was the apple of her father's eye.**

Queen Mary Bimbo, with her trademark pipe
and a young daughter, in one of her
frequent court appearances, this one in 1931.

King Tene at the age of seventy-four.

Steve Tene a few years ago, in his late teens. At that time he had left his family and was chauffeuring *boojo* women around the country. (Photo: From the author's collection)

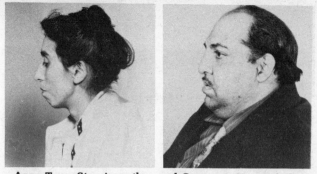

Anna Tene, Steve's mother, and Carranza, Steve's father.

King Tene Bimbo (*hat in hand*) in Chicago during the Depression, leading a funeral cortege for a member of his gypsy tribe.

Steve Tene today, with his grandfather's ring and medallion.
(Photo: Dan Wynn)

able jobs, going to school. . . . But we also have the renegade gypsies—those who are out to swindle the people by claiming they have a gift from God to remove sorrow, sickness, pain and bad luck. That's why we have National Gypsy Crime Investigators, Inc."

A look into the outfit by the New York Police Department and law-enforcement agencies elsewhere soon showed that while it was incorporated in Louisiana, as claimed, it was a fraud dreamed up by members of the Adams tribe to prey on their fellow gypsies. Some agencies, however, were not so alert and promptly sent back information about gypsies sought on specific charges, whereupon National Gypsy Crime Investigators, Inc., did indeed track them down but only to extort money from them; if the "wanted" gypsies did not pay up, they were told that they would be turned over to the law.

Detective Coyne had more or less put the whole business behind him when the revelations of Patrolman, later Detective, Frank Serpico about widespread corruption in the New York Police Department led to the formation of the so-called Knapp Commission to investigate these charges. The commission's probe was making headlines daily and had the police department in a turmoil. One day a request from the Knapp Commission came through official channels to the pickpocket and confidence squad asking for, among other things, a list of pending cases involving gypsies. Coyne complied with the request, and the material was forwarded to the commission. Although Coyne declines to talk about it, there was great consternation in the squad about this turn of events. Nobody knew where the ax was going to fall; what *was* known was that gypsies were always making accusations about law-enforcement corruption and police harassment, and given the atmosphere in New York at the time, it was anybody's guess how far they could go with such charges now.

Nothing further, however, was heard from the commission. But then, in July 1971, Coyne received another communication from National Gypsy Crime Investigators, Inc., addressed personally to him, although misspelling his name "Coin," and it was a good deal tougher than the one which had crossed his desk a year before. It announced that the organization had been working "under the Knapp Commission." It said, "Through our investigations we have found that there is over a half million dollars worth of complaints against gypsies in the City of New York. . . . We know that no arrests have yet been made at this time and we have found that many of the gypsies on whom the complaints are issued have moved away." The organization once again offered its help in finding them and included in the letter a list of gypsies who were wanted and the reasons why they were being sought.

But this time the Adams tribesmen, and whoever they got to write the letter, had overreached themselves. The list was word for word the same as the one Coyne had supplied to the Knapp Commission. And it became immediately clear that a new and devious Romany scheme was in the works. As noted by a television reporter who broke the story to the general embarrassment of the Knapp Commission, gypsies had apparently gone to commission investigators with tales of police corruption, gotten the commission to obtain the desired information from the police department and then used it in a renewed attempt not only to shake down other gypsies but to intimidate the cops as well.

Like his predecessors in the job, Coyne is cynical about gypsies but nonetheless fascinated by them. He has his own alphabet to keep them manageably in mind. "A" is for Adams, "B" is for Bimbo, "C" is for Costello, "D" is for Demetro, "E" is for Evans, and so on down the line until "U" for Uwanowich, "V" for Vlado, "W" for Wanko and Williams, and "Y" for Yonkovich. Much of his time is spent on *boojo* swindles, and he has a sneaking admiration for the way gypsy women are able to pull them off. The success of any good con hinges on taking the victim where he wants to go, and as Coyne says, "These women are very, very good. You can even go in there knowing it's a setup, and they'll have you unstrung in minutes. Sometimes when they're operating like that, I think they believe it themselves."

Boojo women are forever refining their act, and Coyne has observed a new development in the handkerchief-switch phase of the swindle. Instead of substituting the handkerchief with sheaves of paper for the one containing the real money, some *boojo* women will now replace, say, hundred-dollar denominations with one-dollar bills. This enables them to tell a victim that he may reach every now and then into the handkerchief or bag, as the case may be, and reassure himself that the money is still there by actually fingering what is obviously stacks of cash, but under no circumstances, they warn, can the victim look at the bills; otherwise he will go blind. The power a good *boojo* woman commands is enormous. Even when a sucker came to Coyne with suspicions that she had been swindled out of her life savings and brought him to the safe deposit box where a handkerchief supposedly holding the money was being kept, she was afraid to open the handkerchief and look inside it herself. "You do it," she told Coyne. "You look."

And though nothing really fazes Detective Coyne when it comes to gypsies, there are moments that do give him pause. A psychologist once went to him to report that she had gone into an *ofisa* to convince a friend that it was all a sham and had wound up losing some of her jewelry. How, Coyne could not help inquiring, was it possible for a college-educated, seemingly sophisticated person, who was a psychologist to boot, to fall for something like this? "Well," the victim replied, "what can I say? That gypsy was just a better psychologist than me."

Aunt Hazel is a Bimbo. She is also a retired *boojo* woman and one, as she is fond of pointing out, who was never caught at it. Although she has heard of larger scores, the biggest Aunt Hazel ever made herself was thirty-one thousand dollars. It was a burn-up, and quite successful by most standards, but the memory of it still rankles in Aunt Hazel. Her victim, a woman of Nordic descent, was supposed to bring fifty thousand dollars to have the curse removed. "I trusted her for the other nineteen thousand," Aunt Hazel told me, "and she never came back."

"Anyway," I said, "you came out ahead."

"Naturally," she said in an impatient tone indicating that any other possibility was unthinkable.

When I asked Aunt Hazel what the woman's problem was, her recollection suddenly grew vague, as if she were unwilling to be pinned down to traceable specifics. "She was a widow, you know, and she felt something was wrong with her, but she couldn't place her hand on what it was. And I told her the thing that she can't place her hand on was the evil 'cause she was crossed up with money and the money was evil, and to burn the money and throw off the curse so she would get peace of mind and not feel anything is wrong any more."

I expressed amazement that someone could be brought to the point of allowing that much money to be burned. Aunt Hazel chuckled and made it sound simple. "She had two choices. She could destroy her life or the money. Besides, it wasn't money that was being burned up, it was paper."

"But the woman thought it was money."

"Yes, well, that shows you how crazy some people are. Don't forget, there's a sucker every minute, and the hand is quicker than the eye."

Now that she is retired, Aunt Hazel spends her afternoons next to the bay window of her house in the New York City borough of Queens watching the street scene, a habit from her days in an *ofisa*. She is a short, ponderously fat woman, perhaps sixty, widowed herself, with a pear-shaped face and anthracite eyes. Her voice is deep and cadenced, and if she should ever tell me to burn money in a handkerchief, I am sure I would do it instantly.

She won't give an inch on the gypsies. "All right," she said with a massive shrug, "it's true that we steal with the hands, but you *gadje*—you Americans—*you* steal with the pencils." Her voice rose. "And how many gypsies you see going to jail for twenty, fifty years for murderings and rapings and muggings?"

Aunt Hazel, who says she was born in Detroit, remembers traveling around the country in horse-and-wagon caravans, and she recalls what she describes as the constant jeopardy gypsies felt they were in. "We feared, gentleman," she said. "How can I explain it to you? What I know to the best of my knowledge, and what I heard from my own ancestors, we the gypsy people feared from the white people the way the white people here used to fear from the red faces, from the Indians with the feathers, the way you people were scared that they would cut the scalps off the white people."

She paused to quell her emotions. "Yes, gentleman," she said. "I recall those times well. Your people hated us because we were wanderers and loved the fresh air and lived in tents. You people don't want no tents, you don't want fresh air. You want apartments and big buildings, and when we would look up on those buildings, we used to be in fear. Yes, I recall how we would come into a town and the people yelled, 'Lock the doors, the gypsies are coming! Get the children inside, they're going to steal our children.' But I recall how those people yelled too, 'Kill the gypsies, run them out of town, burn them, put them on fire!' Yes, those are my memories."

"You really heard people say things like that?"

"Oh God," she sobbed, "don't make me cry."

Aunt Hazel said the reason gypsies refuse to send their children to *gadjo* schools is very simple. "They'd just get the hell beat out of them, like always." And even if this were not the case, she takes a dim view of the kind of education they would receive. "They'd learn about narcotics," she said, "and mixing people up. Gentleman, I got to tell you we would struggle, we would die, we'd be crucified like Jesus, if we would see our girls go out with black men. You people see that day and night, and you laugh like it's nothing. Shame! Maybe everything goes today, but believe me, the gypsy still has got a little pride left."

According to Aunt Hazel, any gypsy who thinks he can assimilate with the rest of the population—with the *gadje*—is kidding himself. "We the gypsy people have a saying," she growled, "that you can never let a *gadjo* get behind your back. Out of a hundred *gadje* one will say, 'I feel for the gypsy,' but the rest say, 'The hell with the goddamn gypsies. They're ignorant, they're wanderers.' You people even recognized the Chinamen. You got them into the United Nations. What do you do for the poor gypsy?"

The thought of all those Orientals roaming the halls of the UN seemed to rekindle her fury. "Yes," she said, "China got her flag up there, and you let her. Red Russia got her man in there too. When you people think that for better than hundreds of years we're suffering, would you people think of giving us a little recognition, a flag or something, a little kindness? Why, they have Catholic schools, Protestant schools, public schools, private schools, Greek schools! Why couldn't you give us just one little gypsy village school? We don't even get a broken-down barn."

Aunt Hazel can make it sound as if the *gadjo* world were at fault when she went out picking pockets as a girl. "So I took two-twenty-odd dollars from the man," she said, recalling one such incident. "My mother was very sick, and there were a lot of mouths, you know, that were starving, and things were bad, those were hard times, no coal to put in the stove, no groceries, no rent, and I went and stole. But I didn't hit nobody over the head."

She reserves a special bitterness for the police, who, she claims, spend all their time harassing gypsies and shaking them down. Her animosity stems from the time when members of the Bimbo tribe were staying in Chicago and the police rousted all the adults, for some reason she says she cannot remember, and took them away, leaving the children in a house alone. "We were kids, you know what I mean, who were left," she said, "and we were playing around, and one of the youngest, little Mitzi, maybe she was three, four years old, went into the kitchen, and she was playing with a loaf of bread with the wrapping paper on it, and she pressed the button of the stove. The stove was the kind that you don't use no match on, it has a pilot, and she pressed the button, and the flame came up and it got the paper and from the paper all the things she had on got on fire. We tried to kill the flames, but she got all burned up." Aunt Hazel wiped a tear from her eye at the memory of what had occurred, although it took place more than fifty years ago. She is, however, quite correct about the details of the child's death. A one-paragraph item in the Chicago *Tribune,* dated May 1, 1923, reported, "Mitzi Bimbo, 4 years old . . . was fatally burned last night when her dress caught fire from a flame in a stove in her house at 1411 South Halsted St. She died at the Mercy hospital three hours later."

Both as a Bimbo and as a sort of clearinghouse for gypsy gossip at her permanent station in Queens, Aunt Hazel knew all about Steve Tene's arrival from California and how he had taken his sister Sonia out of the hospital in New Jersey after she had attempted suicide. "That was a sorrowful thing, terrible, what the girl did," she said. "But her father Carranza, he's a sick man, you know what I mean, he ain't right in the head. He ain't like his father, who was the King of Kings."

At the thought of King Tene Bimbo, the tribe's late patriarch, Aunt Hazel grew rhapsodic. "Yes, *there* was a man," she told me. "At the age of fifteen, believe me, he had the brain of a fifty-year-old, and when our various tribes had trouble among themselves, when the older people couldn't settle it, they would come to him and listen to his words and look upon what he said and follow it because it was always right. When he was just maybe ten, eleven years old, everybody knows this, there was a trial between gypsies and he just sat there taking it in, and that trial went on for three days and three nights. And there was this wise old man running the trial and he noticed the boy staying there all that time and the old man went up to him and said, 'What is your name?' and he said, 'My name is Tene.' And the old man said, 'What do you think about this? I've been watching you very closely—you, a young boy who has been listening to what's been happening here, what do you think, who is to blame?' So Tene said, 'Well, this person says so-and-so time and so-and-so place, and then the other person said these words'— and he repeated it, everything that had been said—and then he said, 'Therefore I find this person guilty.' And the old man took him by the hand and said, 'Tene, I can see that you are going to be a very, very smart man, a king among men, when you grow up,' and the old man had said this 'cause the same person the boy had found guilty, the trial had found guilty too."

It was not only Tene Bimbo's wisdom, according to Aunt Hazel, that had him acclaimed king but also his generosity, "the way," as she put it, "he used to bring hungry gypsies food, the way he used to take them to the hospitals to get them cured, the way he used to try to rent them houses to live in or rent them fields where they could camp and bring them wood and water and feed their horses."

I asked Aunt Hazel if she was talking about all the tribes or just the Bimbos, and she bridled with indignation. "All the gypsy tribes recognized him," she insisted, "the Stevensons and the Thompsons, the Adamses, the Williams tribe and the Evans tribe and the Greens and the Uwanowiches, the Demetros, all them people. When they heard the name King Tene Bimbo, they are just like numb, they feared from that name. I don't care what they say. They might say different behind his back but when they faced him, they shivered and lost their tongues."

When I suggested that this did not quite square with the portrait she had painted of a universally respected and admired leader, she replied with sweet reasonableness, "Well, 'course he was tough, he was a Bimbo, you know, and he was hard, a killer too. 'Cause he had to be. In the beginning it was the way I explained, but time goes on and he grew in power and there were tribes like the Kaslovs and the Mitchells which were jealous of him and tried to frame him with the police and put him down, and he had to deal with them, you know what I mean, and he did deal with them."

What about King Tene's grandson Steve, I asked, and the changes he was trying to bring to the gypsy life? She said, "I will tell you honestly and truthfully. Stevie is my blood, but he's a young, mixed-up boy who was brought up in fear 'cause of his father. And with all his Americanization, and what he tells me of the American people, that we're wrong about them, that we never went to them to explain ourselves, I told him, 'Stevie, you're young. You don't know our history, what we went through for hundreds of years, what your grandfather, what *my* father and *his* father and *his* father's father went through.' I told Stevie that's something you can't wash out in ten minutes."

Aunt Hazel's dogma faltered for the first time in her attempt to explain why King Tene Bimbo had selected Steve to succeed him. "Well, gentleman," she said, "I can't lie. Many of our tribe cried and were in shock when we heard this, but the old man was the King of Kings and maybe he saw something or felt something of what Stevie would mean for the new generation 'cause the old man was known for his sharp eye and strong mind." And as if in bewildered testament to changing times which she does not entirely comprehend, she suddenly interjected, "I own this house, you know. I even pay taxes on it."

Like most gypsies her age, however, Aunt Hazel is certain that Steve will die in the end at the hand of his father. "With all this talk of Stevie's about giving our children schooling and freedom," she said, "Carranza thinks Stevie is violating the gypsy law. He feels that Stevie is betraying our many tribes by trying to Americanize them for the benefit of the *gadje*. That's what he's going around telling everybody."

Aunt Hazel shifted her great bulk on a red velvet sofa protected by a plastic slipcover. "Besides," she added ominously, "like I say, Carranza ain't right in the head. You saw what he had done, tried to have done, to Stevie's eyes with the knife. Stevie got the ring and the medallion, and Carranza believes that this was a glory that belongs to him. If the old man, our king, hadn't died, none of this trouble would of happened."

PART
III

❦

The King

King Tene Bimbo—feared and loathed by rival tribes, venerated and slavishly followed by his own clan—was eighty-five when he went into Park East, a small, private hospital in Manhattan. "One of his daughters phoned," Aunt Hazel recalled, "and said it's nothing, he's just going in for a checkup, and maybe five, six days later he was gone."

He was admitted to Park East at 7:15 in the evening on October 14, 1969. He was then far removed from the terrorizing figure he had once been to so many gypsies, white-haired now, bent over so that he appeared even shorter than his normal five-feet-four, and he was so obese, weighing nearly two hundred fifty pounds, that in his initial examination his liver, spleen and kidneys could not be felt. For about two months he had been ailing and twice had visited a doctor complaining of chest pains, for which he received anticongestive medication for his heart. By October 13 his condition had deteriorated to the point where hospitalization was required. But the night he went into Park East he had no obvious discomfort other than swollen ankles. According to his medical records, he expressed concern about his liver, having knocked off at least a fifth of rye a day for as long as he could remember.

Amazingly enough, however, when his liver was finally probed, it was only minimally enlarged and was not at all tender. He had no fever, and the admission diagnosis was that he was suffering from hardening of the arteries and was a prime candidate for congestive heart failure. He had a private room and around-the-clock private nurses paid for a week in advance, along with a deposit covering estimated laboratory and other expenses, in cash.

His second day was taken up with tests, during which he remained about the same. The third day he took a slight turn for the worse with abdominal pain and vomiting; an electrocardiogram also revealed that he had suffered a "previous myocardial infarction," or heart attack, although he claimed to have no knowledge of it. On October 17 he seemed to be better, still had no fever, said he felt no pain, and some difficulty he had experienced in breathing disappeared.

By then Bimbos and their allies were swarming in from all over the country—from Boston, Philadelphia, Baltimore, Chicago and Cleveland, from St. Louis, Kansas City and Dallas, Los Angeles and San Francisco. They poured by the scores into Park East. "I never saw anything like it," a security guard told me. "It didn't matter what time it was, night or day, they just barged in." They came not only to visit but to stay, crowding the corridors outside his room, overflowing the reception areas, some setting up house on the spot, more sleeping in cars parked for blocks around the hospital. Finally the police had to be summoned to maintain at least a show of order.

When Aunt Hazel saw King Tene, she asked him what was wrong, and he said, "I'm tired," and she, blinking back her tears, said, "You're good for another fifty years," and he whispered, "I don't think so." He then told each assemblage gathered around his bed, in a tone markedly more subdued than the one they were used to hearing, "I want you all to understand what I'm telling you. I want you to forget what was done to me in the past. Forgive and forget. Whoever was my enemy, let God be his judge. Don't hold grudges inside or outside our tribe. Try to get along with each other. Let bygones be bygones."

It was an uncharacteristic call from the old man, who had a criminal record featuring more than one hundred and twenty-five arrests on such felonious matters as grand larceny, extortion, attempted murder, robbery, kidnapping, assault and battery, perjury, inciting to riot and bank theft in, among other states, Illinois, Massachusetts, Michigan, New York, Tennessee, Texas, Minnesota, Wisconsin, New Jersey and California, as well as the District of Columbia. Some of these charges involved crimes committed, as they say, against society, but others, particularly those concerning extortion and kidnapping, often appear on gypsy "rap sheets" as part of the constant internecine feuding that goes on among many Romany tribes. If a clan, for whatever reason, feels aggrieved by another, it has become common to bypass a *kris* and to go into court with trumped-up accusations that are usually countered by ones that are equally phony. A "kidnapping" may prove to be nothing more than a dispute over a girl's bridal price, and "extortion" charges are another convenient method of settling scores. As a Chicago judicial notice pointed out a half-century ago, "In any case in which one gypsy testifies against another . . . most of our judges here at one time or another have become acquainted with the trickeries of these people and would be very hesitant about believing them unless there was some corroborative evidence from other persons."

Tene Bimbo was always embroiled in controversies like these as he clawed his way to power. One of the earliest on record occurred in 1911 in Kenosha, Wisconsin, where he was listed as "Toma Bimble." It was charged that he "did rob, steal and carry away with force and violence one thousand dollars" from another gypsy. Having made bail, he promptly disappeared. He turned up again in 1914 in St. Cloud, Minnesota, on a similar charge as "John Poluth" with the same result. Even now, with all the modern detection tools available to law-enforcement agencies, it is difficult enough to find a gypsy who wants to drop out of sight; in those days it was practically impossible and, indeed, most municipalities were delighted to have the whole thing go away. A gypsy named Mike Frank swore that in Cleveland in 1917 King Tene along with other armed Bimbos invaded a house occupied by members of the Frank clan and made off with jewelry and gold coins. Also in 1917, according to the affidavit of another gypsy, Pete Williams, Tene Bimbo braced him in Detroit and demanded five hundred dollars. Williams said he asked what the money was for, and Tene replied, "All the gypsies give me money and you got to give me money too." Williams said that he refused to knuckle under, whereupon King Tene had Queen Mary swear out a warrant accusing Williams of hitting her on the head with a brick and stealing a gold necklace. "I learned that Tene Bimbo had someone hit his wife so that he could claim I did it," Williams said. The depositions of Frank and Williams came some years after the fact; both men claimed that they had not pressed charges at the time because they feared further retribution from the Bimbos. There are dozens of similar incidents dotting King Tene's career. Theodore Stevenson and Steve Bacho, when they incurred his displeasure, said they were accused by him of raping and robbing one of his daughters; Miller and Ephram Frank were supposedly robbed of fifteen hundred dollars at pistol point; a Tucon Miller had to pay a thousand dollars or Tene Bimbo would "give me a ride and kill me"; it was alleged that King Tene regularly held mass meetings of gypsies to collect tribute, the minimum "donation" being fifty dollars; Joe and John Nicholas claimed that when they declined to pay Tene a thousand dollars, he and various other Bimbos entered their house, broke open a trunk and helped themselves to twenty-five hundred dollars in cash and jewelry; Eli Urich swore that Tene Bimbo had come to his house while he was away, took two hundred dollars from his wife, and then, when Urich's "little brother" protested, "threatened him with an iron poker if he tried to call any assistance or make any outcry."

While some of these depositions were undoubtedly as false as those which King Tene himself used to swear to, even the Bimbos admit that the old man had a predilection for demanding—and collecting—money. The difference in opinion concerned his purpose, which according to the Bimbos was profoundly noble. "With all the bad things he did in his life," one of them told me, "he did mostly good, uh, like Rockefeller or them other big people the *gadje* go to when you need help and you ask them for money. Maybe a tribe of the Greens or Stokes or Evans are in trouble, or a gypsy got hurt or had a misunderstanding or his wife went away or he didn't have no money to get a house or a store— well, that gypsy, he would come to King Tene, and King Tene would make, you know what I mean, a collection for him. King Tene would go to gypsies with money, and if they would say, 'It's his hard luck, let him take care of himself,' King Tene would say, 'You think you're a big man! I'll show you how small you are. Give me the money or I'll cut your tongue out, I'll break your fucking legs!' Believe me, he wasn't fooling. If he had to do it, he did it."

This benevolent view was not shared by, among others, the Illinois state's attorney for Cook County, Chicago's equivalent of a district attorney, who had to contend with King Tene and his followers throughout the 1920s and early 1930s. "The Bimbos and their entire family and relatives," he reported, "have been a source of constant trouble to this office, and it has been our experience that they cannot be believed under any circumstances."

King Tene Bimbo, along with Queen Mary, settled on Chicago as his headquarters around 1920. In marrying her in Yonkers, New York, in 1905, he had helped to broaden his power base and potential alliances, since she came from an important branch of the Muchwaya gypsies, who regard their Kalderash brethren, with whom the Bimbos are tribally affiliated, as distinctly blue-collar types. When he arrived in Chicago, the leading gypsy in the city was King Eli Miguel, and within a year Tene took him on, swearing out a warrant that King Eli and two others had assaulted a helpless Bimbo female and ripped off her person a gold necklace composed of twenty-five twenty-dollar gold pieces. Emerging from police court, where he had demanded immediate justice, Tene told an assemblage of journalists, "Eli Miguel, he is not the king. He is the bunk! *I* am the King of the Gypsies." In so saying, as one reporter described it, Tene patted himself on the chest in a manner that was "lordly, but restrained." It was further noted that King Eli, when last seen, was headed "posthaste toward the Indiana border."

Consolidating his position in the ensuing months, Tene Bimbo was constantly in and out of court. He had a canny sense of public relations, and reporters were always on hand for one of his appearances. While most gypsies could not read the fine print in the newspapers, they recognized his picture and could pick out his name in the headlines, all of which only served to boost his prestige in the Romany community. Once, on his way to still another hearing, he announced on the courthouse steps that his royal responsibilities were a heavy burden and that thus far his legal fees amounted to nearly two hundred thousand dollars.

"What's the charge this time, King?" a reporter asked.

"Mayhem," Tene replied, adding with a grin, "I don't even know what it means. I ain't so good in English. So besides paying the lawyers, I got to buy—what you call it?—a dictionary to find out what I'm here for."

King Tene's next big splash in the Chicago press occurred in 1924. The complainant against him was Amelia "Queen Millie" Marks, one of the few gypsy matriarchs in her own right, who headed a relatively small but aggressive band of gypsies that had remained independent of his sway in the city. According to

Queen Millie, she paid Tene Bimbo $2,250 to let his daughter Rose, then fourteen, marry one of her sons, George. After handing over the agreed-upon sum, she said, the wedding took place, but a few hours after the ceremony her new daughter-in-law vanished without so much as a word, and Queen Millie accused King Tene of plotting the whole affair to swindle her out of the money. He responded at once with a charge of his own that George Marks, the alleged bridegroom, and a brother had in fact assaulted and raped poor Rose. Queen Millie, giving no quarter, then swore out a second warrant against Tene, accusing him of having her beaten up for trying to retrieve her money.

As it turned out, this second charge by Queen Millie went to court first, and King Tene was acquitted. It apparently filled him with a false sense of security, for in the main event that followed, the trial concerning the money, he offered nothing more than a general denial by him and Rose, backed up by some gypsies who attested to his "good character," while Queen Millie paraded in witness after witness who swore they were present during the marital negotiations, when the cash was paid, at the wedding and in the house when Rose suddenly disappeared. Finally sensing that things were not going well for him, King Tene had his lawyer make a last-minute call for another trial because of new evidence. But it was too late. The judge refused and sent the case to the jury. During the seven hours the jurors were out, the tension among the waiting gypsies exploded, and more than a hundred of them, minions of either King Tene or Queen Millie, went at each other in the courthouse corridors. Several squads of cops were required to separate the combatants, and eleven gypsies were hospitalized for injuries inflicted by Romany brass knuckles and knives or police night sticks.

King Tene, to his anguish, was found guilty and was sentenced to a prison term of from one to ten years. He appealed. When the appeal reached the Illinois State Supreme Court some months later, the rape case against the brothers Marks was still pending because of postponements instigated by Tene's attorney, and this served to cloud the issue. In addition King Tene unveiled his new evidence—another suitor for Rose's hand from whom, he swore, he had received twenty-five hundred dollars long before Queen Millie entered the picture, thus making it impossible, in compliance with "long-standing gypsy tradition, custom and law," for him to have concluded any marital deal with her for his daughter. Rose's truly betrothed, it was explained, had been kept under wraps until now to save him from being involved publicly in such a sordid matter. The august justices considered the dizzying array of claims and counterclaims and depositions totally at odds with one another and finally threw up their collective hands in despair and ordered a second trial.

The real story, according to members of the Bimbo tribe who were there at the time, was that King Tene for once was not completely at fault. The actual culprit was Rose, the "apple of his eye," his first-born daughter, spoiled, headstrong and a beauty. "Even the *gadje,* the American people, you know," one of them said, "would stop and turn around and stare just by the sight of her walking down the street." And it was because of this, they say, that Queen Millie kept after King Tene to give up Rose to her son, arguing that among other things such an alliance would end any more bickering over who dominated Chicago's gypsies. "Mention any price you want," Queen Millie allegedly said, "and it's yours."

The problem was that the willful Rose wanted nothing to do with Queen Millie's son, and King Tene remained hesitant. Then, I was told, "Millie said she would give two, three thousand dollars for Rosie, which was big money in them days, and the old man thought it over and said, 'All right,' never thinking Millie would do it, that she was bluffing, but she did, and there was nothing he could do. So they made the wedding, and after it was over Rosie just walked out of the house in her wedding dress about one o'clock in the morning and came back to him and said she ain't leaving and she don't care what happens. And the old man, who wasn't happy about what he had done anyway, said he would stand by her, and that's how the trouble started."

The second trial was never held. Apparently shaken by the reversal of Tene Bimbo's conviction, Queen Millie forsook further prosecution in return for his dropping the rape charges against her sons. As part of the settlement he agreed to hand back half the bridal price she had paid for Rose, but it is questionable whether he ever did, since he also agreed not to "molest or harm the Marks family in the future," and then proceeded to pick them off one by one and run them out of Chicago until Queen Millie herself at last fled the city for more amicable surroundings.

In 1928 King Tene, seeking new worlds to rule, turned his eyes eastward, specifically toward Boston, where two rivals, Joseph Mitchell and Pete Thompson, were the major figures in the gypsy community. He left Chicago in late May in a large black Lincoln sedan driven by his son Pete, then twenty, who dressed and looked like a young Al Capone and acted as his father's bodyguard and chauffeur. Also in the car were Queen Mary, puffing as usual on her long-stemmed pipe, daughter Rose and several Bimbo small fry. Other carloads of Bimbos were to follow.

According to the Bimbo version of the ensuing events, they were innocently heading along a Massachusetts turnpike on the way to Boston when King Tene suddenly said, "Pete, slow down. Looks like there's a gypsy camp up there," and Pete replied, "Yeah, you're right. Let's see what's going on. Boston ain't far, and we'll make it there before night anyway."

King Tene, in fact, knew perfectly well what was going on. What he claimed to have spotted with such astonishment was a huge gypsy encampment, of the kind no longer seen in this country, on a dairy farm owned by some brothers named Dooley near the Massachusetts mill town of Methuen, about thirty miles north of Boston, and not at all on any highway one would normally take, then or now, driving from Chicago. Gypsies tend to seize upon almost any holiday, whether their own or somebody else's—be it Christmas, Easter, the Fourth of July or even the Jewish New Year, Rosh Hashana—as a cause for celebration. In this instance, it was May 29, the eve of Memorial Day, and more than three hundred of them, embracing members of a half-dozen tribes in and around Boston, had already erected tents on approximately five acres of meadowland rented from the Dooley brothers. It was an idyllic location, a harkening back to a Romany past rapidly being eclipsed, the grassy field, dotted with trees, sweeping down to a clear, swift-flowing tributary of the Merrimack River.

Before King Tene left Chicago, an ally of his, a gypsy named Wasso Wonko, had advised him of the encampment and its location. Wonko was there, as was a grouping of the Johns tribe, also friendly to Tene, along with unsuspecting Mitchells, Thompsons, Millers, Williamses and Franks, among others. King Tene's Lincoln roared up a dirt road past what police and reporters would later describe as dozens of parked Lincolns, LaSalles, Cadillacs and Pierce-Arrows, mostly touring cars. As the Bimbos tell it, King Tene stepped out of his car and said expansively to the gypsies who had gathered around him, "Ah, good afternoon. Whose tribes are these here?"

A gypsy whom the Bimbos would identify as Joseph Mitchell replied, "What difference whose tribes are here? You won't have time to see them."

King Tene, according to the Bimbos, professed not to hear this. "Do you people know who I am?" he said. "Are you giving me an honor? Did you people know I was coming or passing through?"

"We heard you might be coming," Mitchell was supposed to have said. "We're having a big feast here, but the feast is not for you. This is going to be your funeral." With that he and some of the other gypsies began to move menacingly toward him, and King Tene backed to his car and whispered to Queen Mary, "Hand me my gun."

The version offered by some of the gypsies encamped at the Dooley farm differed considerably from this. The meeting, they claimed, had actually been called by Tene Bimbo, and they had come out of curiosity. When he rolled up in his Lincoln and got out, he announced to the assemblage that he intended to settle in the East and demanded an immediate tribute of four thousand dollars or he "would make trouble for them." When certain gypsies, notably Mitchells, Williamses and Franks, objected, Tene, they said, went back to his car, reached in the window and pulled out a revolver.

At that point the stories, although there would continue to be great variances in them, at least agreed that this was when the melee began.

Methuen, a mile away, then had a population of about twenty thousand and was situated between the Merrimack Valley industrial centers of Lawrence and Lowell. While the great Wall Street crash of 1929 was a year away, economic distress was already creeping through the valley, and unemployment rolls were mounting. The weather was warm enough for the first straw hats of the summer to have made an appearance, and along with the annual Memorial Day parade, there would be a big event for Methuen ball fans, a game to be played with a team from Kingston in neighboring New Hampshire. For recreation in the evening the Beaver Lake Pavilion and the Bella Vista were featuring "cheek dancing."

The understaffed Methuen police force consisted of twenty men, a request for additional manpower having been denied by the town fathers earlier that year. Joseph R. Hutchinson, a retired police captain now eighty-one years old and still a Methuen resident, remembers the night of the "gypsy riot." Hutchinson had been on the day shift and was "just lounging around" after supper when, at about six o'clock, the emergency call—two blasts, three times—was sounded on the horn outside the Methuen Fire Department. He rushed to police headquarters and was instructed to remain there to coordinate communications. When the Methuen police first reached the scene, Chief Frank Seiferth took one look and realized that he did not have enough men with him to handle the situation. It was starting to get dark, several tents were down, gypsies "were running all over the place," many of them brandishing lengths of two-by-fours and tent poles, and some were wielding swords, and knives were also thought to have been seen glinting, the women and children adding to the general confusion with their hysterical shrieks. Reinforcements were called for through Hutchinson at his post in Methuen, and some fifty cops responded from Lawrence, along with thirty-odd more from Lowell.

At the Dooley farm, according to the Bimbos, as King Tene retreated to his car, Joseph Mitchell said, "Yes, we're going to drain your blood little by little and end all this about you being the king and trying to conquer all our tribes." When Tene asked his wife to pass him the pistol, she allegedly pleaded with him, "Jump in, and we'll back out and make a turn and try to get away."

"There's no chance," he said. "Look, they're behind the car too. They're all around us. Don't talk no more. Just give me the gun." Then, with it finally in hand, he turned to the advancing gypsies and said, "You sons of bitches. If I die, I'm taking a lot of you with me."

The Bimbo tribe views this as the ultimate example of the old man's courage. "He knew," one of them told me, "he was facing death, you know, but he didn't care, he stood his ground and he survived. It's a miracle he lived, why he didn't die right there was a mystery for many years afterwards."

A young Bimbo who was in the car recalls that the hostile gypsies leaped on King Tene, that he went down and then somehow was up again on the running board, and Queen Mary was yelling, "Get in the car! The door's open!" and then he started shooting—"pow, pow, pow!"—and his son Pete put the Lincoln first in forward, then reverse, trying to clear a path for a getaway, but the Mitchells and the others were all over the car swinging clubs and pounding on the roof. The windshield was smashed and next the side windows, and rocks were being thrown as well as pots and pans, and Pete Bimbo at the wheel was telling everyone in the car to duck down. Some of the Johns tribe were fighting on Tene's side, and his friend Wasso Wonko was struggling to get near the car to help him when the old man, blood streaming down his face, finally shouted at Pete, "Let's go! Run them over!" and Pete, obeying instructions, roared forward, and the Lincoln hit somebody—who, it later turned out, was none other than the hapless Wonko—and crashed through a tent. Everybody scattered momentarily, and Pete got the Lincoln turned around, parts of the tent flapping behind it, and started bumping across the meadow, trying to find his way back to the dirt road and the highway, dodging and twisting as most of the camp was again in full chase, blocking his exit, screaming obscenities and hurling whatever objects they could lay their hands on.

The opposing gypsies claimed it was quite the contrary. After King Tene had demanded his tribute and been rebuffed, they said, there was a purely verbal exchange of threats and taunts before Tene went to the car, suddenly turned around holding a pistol and began shooting, one bullet striking Joseph Mitchell, who fell to the ground. Tene Bimbo continued to fire from the running board, and only then did they try to do something to protect themselves. Pete Bimbo—whom they also accused of having a gun and shooting wildly—panicked and in attempting to drive off across the field rammed the Lincoln into a tree, thus causing the injuries that Tene was found to have suffered—a severe concussion, a deep scalp laceration, multiple abrasions of the face, two black eyes, a split lower lip, abrasions of the shoulders and chest and four fractured ribs.

Who summoned the police was never clearly established. The meadow where the fight took place can be easily seen from Route 110, the principal road between Lowell and Lawrence, and a passing motorist might have spotted what was going on, or someone in the Dooley farmhouse could have heard all the noise, although it was a considerable distance from the actual field of battle. The Bimbos credit Rose as the one who initiated help by rushing down to the highway, flagging a car and yelling, "Help, get the police! They're killing my father and mother, my little brothers and sisters, up there!" If so, she immediately returned to the fray, since she was the only female among all the tribesmen arrested that night.

After the police had cordoned off the meadow and restored order, spotlights playing eerily on the scene, a total of fifty-one gypsies were brought to the Methuen police station around 9 P.M. Officer Hutchinson, still manning the desk, had the job of booking them. "It was a nightmare," he recalls. "We only had three cells and when they were full, we started putting them just in a room under armed guard." Even this was not sufficient, and the overflow was removed to police headquarters in Lawrence. While a number of gypsies had assorted cuts and bruises, the only ones taken to the Lawrence General Hospital were Tene Bimbo; Wasso Wonko, who, as a result of Pete Bimbo running over him, had a compound leg fracture and an arm broken in two places; Adolph Johns, who had been shot through the hand; and Joseph Mitchell. Mitchell had a bullet lodged in his chest so close to his heart that it was deemed inoperable at least for the moment; he was listed in critical condition, and early reports held little hope for his recovery. All four men in the hospital were guarded by police while an investigation was launched to try to find out what had happened, although Chief Seiferth in Methuen said with great prescience, after listening to the tangled versions offered by his Romany prisoners, "I doubt if we'll ever get to the bottom of this."

The next day the Methuen police switchboard was jammed with gypsies calling from all over the country inquiring about the fate of relatives and friends, the state of their health and expected period of incarceration. It was incredible, as Hutchinson notes, that they learned about the trouble so fast. And by Friday, June 1, gypsies were flooding into the area, swelling the original encampment, the rest coming into the city itself. Several carloads of Bimbos, who had been following behind King Tene, had already rented rooms, apartments and stores in a downtown section of Methuen. Citizens became unnerved by the sight of so many alien folk wandering through their streets. The Methuen Police Department went on full alert, borrowing additional

cops from Lawrence, and a guard was posted as well at
the Dooley farm. Police were quoted as being particularly worried about the "ugly mood of the gypsy
women," and the city was awash with rumors that
"hordes of gypsies," as yet unseen, were headed for
Methuen. Some of the citizenry began calling for the
National Guard, but the town attorney, Hugh A. Gregg,
sought to reassure them. He was on top of the situation, he said, adding that the Bimbos were responsible
for starting the riot. Rose Bimbo was being charged
with disturbing the peace. Pete Bimbo was being held
in bail of five thousand dollars for assault with a dangerous weapon. Tene Bimbo, once he was released from
the hospital, would be charged with either murder or
attempted murder, depending upon whether Joseph
Mitchell lived or died.

On Friday twenty-seven gypsies were still being held
in lieu of bail of three hundred dollars, fairly stiff in
those days, for disturbing the peace. By Saturday afternoon, all but seven had put up the money, including
Rose Bimbo. "They had plenty of dough," Officer
Hutchinson recalls, "and they either paid in gold coins
or cash. I think the only people in town who were happy were the lawyers. They really cleaned up." Hutchinson was right. More than a dozen local attorneys would
be involved in the case before it was over.

On Sunday special arrangements were made for the
last seven gypsies still in jail for disturbing the peace to
be released upon payment of three-hundred-dollar
bonds, and in the afternoon reporters were permitted
to visit the encampment at the Dooley farm. Although
Methuen Police Chief Seiferth's collection of weapons
picked up at the site included pistols, presumably be-

longing to the Bimbos, hatchets, shotguns, knives and swords, reporters found the camp "tranquil." They were greeted "affably" by Pete Thompson, now in command because of the hospitalization of Joseph Mitchell, who said, "Newspapers? Sure. You want photographs? Take all you want." Thompson led them on a tour of the camp, where they saw "women bent over a rambling brook scrubbing clothes," others "tending pots of pungent food over fires," children "grasping the coattails of cameramen asking to 'see' the pictures" and men "crouched around in circles, smoking and talking quietly." Thompson, according to newspaper reports, then led the visiting journalists into his tent, "the ground covered with tapestries, fur rugs and gaily embroidered pillows," where he emphasized the peacefulness of what they had just observed, noting that it "would always have been like this without Tene Bimbo."

By Wednesday, June 6, Adolph Johns was out of the hospital, Joseph Mitchell was thought to be out of danger, Tene was still hospitalized and Pete Bimbo remained in custody. And the tension that had gripped Methuen began to ease. Gypsies, except for those who had relatives directly involved in court proceedings, were vacating the Dooley farm, and health inspectors started finding violations in the quarters being occupied by the Bimbos in order to drive them out of the town. On Friday an arraignment was held for the principals. Tene Bimbo was well enough to make a brief appearance in court before being returned to the hospital. He was charged with attempted murder with a bail of ten thousand dollars, later reduced to five thousand. Pete Bimbo's bail was lowered upon plea of his lawyer to thirteen hundred dollars, which he promptly put up, and he was released. Eighteen gypsies pleaded *nolo contendere,* and town attorney Gregg informed the presiding judge that he had advised their lawyers that, upon receipt of such a plea, he would recommend their cases be "filed"—in effect, dropped—following payment of court costs. Eight of those arraigned had to supply bail of two hundred dollars as material witnesses. This left seven defendants to be tried: the three Bimbos actively involved in the fight—Tene, Pete and Rose—as well as four gypsies on the other side, all of whom had been countercharged by Tene Bimbo with assault and battery. The date fixed to begin settling these matters was July 13.

But the "mess" which prosecutor Gregg had promised to clear up forthwith was getting messier all the time. The names of the gypsies collared at the farm had been routinely forwarded to other police departments in New England. The results were almost immediate. One was wanted for swindling a Danbury, Connecticut, man out of three thousand dollars; two others were wanted by police for con games in three different Massachusetts cities; two more were being sought by police in Hartford, Connecticut, on a twenty-six-hundred-dollar grand larceny charge; still two others were taken in tow by Boston police for car theft. Tene Bimbo, of course, claimed that any shots he had fired were purely in self-defense. In addition, to complicate things more, he revealed from his hospital bed that he had arrived from Chicago carrying three warrants he had sworn out against gypsies who were in the camp, accusing them of stealing money from him, and he insisted that this was the reason why he had been attacked. He had members of the Bimbo tribe contact the Chicago Police Department, and two detectives duly arrived in Methuen to extradite the wanted trio.

So what had at first appeared to be such a simple case of "good" gypsies versus "bad" gypsies was turning into a quagmire for the town attorney. Joseph Mitchell unwittingly muddied things further by recovering from his gunshot wound, making the situation less clear-cut, less dramatic. And the arrest of so many seemingly innocent victims of the Bimbo attack by out-of-town police, together with all of King Tene's legal maneuvering, led to another frustrating roadblock for Gregg. The gypsies were clamming up. As he would inform the court with more than a little exasperation, "It is becoming impossible to prosecute these complaints, since all the defendants apparently have patched up the differences which led to the quarrel and are now refusing to take the witness stand to testify."

Joseph Mitchell alone was adamant about pressing charges. And by the end of June both he and Tene were out of the hospital, but what Methuen really wanted was to get rid of the gypsies once and for all. This was reflected in the prosecutor's quick agreement on July 13 to a continuance of the case for at least two months, using as an excuse the incapacity of the unfortunate Wasso Wonko, the one true loser in the affair, whose leg had been so mangled that for a while amputation was considered. King Tene's bail was reduced to two thousand dollars, which he had no problem putting up, and finally in September the matter was handed over to a grand jury. The grand jury deliberated with glacial speed, and another year passed before it voted to indict —nobody.

While the grand jury was in session, King Tene, after

a brief sojourn in Chicago, was busy beating an extortion rap against him in Detroit and a perjury indictment in Tennessee, where it seemed that he had falsely charged some Memphis gypsies with having robbed him. In the summer of 1929 he again turned eastward to Pennsylvania, where the Miller tribe occupied a dominant position. What Tene wanted besides a lump-sum tribute was a cut in the fortune-telling operation that the Millers ran in various cities, amusement parks and carnivals throughout the state. In Philadelphia Tene had a meeting with the tribe's chief, Thomas Miller, who laughed at him. Subsequently there was a midnight raid on Miller gypsies during which they were beaten, their tents burned and twenty-eight hundred dollars taken. At a second meeting Miller, in his anger, made the mistake of calling Tene a "pretender" to the Romany throne and a "bastard fake." King Tene forgot all about the money and unleashed an onslaught of savagery unprecedented even by his standards. In Harrisburg a Miller tribesman was clubbed so viciously that he was paralyzed from the waist down. In quick succession two others were ambushed and murdered by unidentified assailants. But this time Tene did not make the same error as in Methuen—he never personally involved himself in these assaults and, indeed, was not to be found in the state. In midsummer Thomas Miller was ensconced in an amusement park near Hazleton, about a hundred miles northwest of Philadelphia, when what he described as "strange gypsies" began showing up around his concession. He went to the police for protection but by then was so cowed that he could not bring himself to mention Tene Bimbo by name, characterizing him instead as "someone from Chicago." The cops on the basis of this could do little, although the amusement park agreed to beef up its security force. For a few days Miller watched nervously while more strange gypsies made inquiries among other concessionaires about him and how much he might be making, and finally at 1:30 A.M. on August 10, according to police and news reports, he suddenly packed up with his followers and fled not only Hazleton but Pennsylvania.

Satisfied that he had left a calling card the Millers would not soon forget, King Tene next popped up in Methuen, where he heard the glad tidings that the grand jury had not indicted him, and then headed for the West Coast, which, as far as any official records are concerned, he had not yet visited. In Los Angeles he continued his particular brand of extortion—once being accused of theft by a gypsy who, after thinking it over, abruptly decided not to follow through on his accusation—and then went to San Francisco. He had just arrived when he received disquieting news from Chicago. One of Tene Bimbo's routine sources of income was payoffs from all *ofisas* operating in the city whether he was physically in residence or not, and he now learned that during his absence another gypsy, Angelo Nichols, had started up a string of them and was openly defying this enforced tribute.

King Tene hurried back to Chicago and cornered Nichols. In addition to regular payments commencing immediately, he also demanded five thousand dollars. Nichols said no, whereupon three of his *ofisas,* one after another, were bombed out. In a follow-up confrontation Tene told Nichols that the next target, unless he came up with the money, would be not one of his *ofisas* but Nichols himself. Shortly thereafter a bullet whizzed through a window of the house Nichols lived in. This was too much for Nichols, who scurried to the state's attorney with the whole story of King Tene's extortion attempts and threat to kill him.

The prosecutor's office was beside itself with joy. For about a decade it had been trying to nail Tene Bimbo without success, and at long last victory was in sight. With the cooperation of Nichols, an elaborate scheme was devised to put King Tene behind bars. First he was brought in for questioning, during the course of which it was let slip that Angelo Nichols not only was talking but would be the state's main witness against him. After Tene had been released, informants relayed word that he was going around looking, as Patrick Roche, the chief investigator for the state's attorney, put it, for an "avenging agent" to silence Nichols for good. That was exactly what everybody had wanted. Roche assigned an undercover man to approach King Tene in a restaurant he frequented. The disguised detective said he had heard that Tene was in the market for someone to do a job for him. "I'll give two-fifty to have a man bumped off," Tene Bimbo replied without hesitation.

"I know a man who'll take the job," the detective said, "but it may cost you a little more."

King Tene waved his hand contemptuously, as though money were no object; the important thing, he said, was that the job be done well and with dispatch. The undercover man introduced Tene to the supposed killer, a second detective working for the state's attorney, who, to make the plot more plausible, held out for a five-hundred-dollar fee. Tene agreed but added a proviso: he had to know exactly when the murder was to be committed. A couple of days later he was given a time and place for that afternoon. All during this period he had been kept under close surveillance, and the reason for his desiring advance notice became apparent. Soon after he received the call, he and two of his sons walked into a Chicago police station on some pretext and remained there while the killing was allegedly taking place, thus giving himself what he presumed to be a perfect alibi. The police, in turn, used his presence in the station house to their own advantage by sending in a report that Nichols had been found slain.

King Tene then met the hired assassin for the payoff but threw everyone into momentary panic when he declared that he desired further proof; he wanted to see the body. So Angelo Nichols had to be rushed to the city morgue and laid out on a slab under a sheet for a quick viewing.

Finally convinced that the usurper to his power had gone to his ultimate reward, Tene Bimbo reverted to type and started haggling over the price, knocking it down to two hundred and eighty dollars, and was promptly arrested for conspiracy to murder. An internal memo in the office of the state's attorney described it as a "perfect conspiracy case," and chief investigator Roche told the press that everything had been carefully monitored from beginning to end with witnesses to all the key conversations, as well as to the money changing hands. It was, he said, "airtight."

But King Tene was not finished yet. He waived a jury trial, and his lawyer argued in court that if he was going to be a defendant on this charge, the two undercover men ought to be prosecuted with equal vigor; they, after all, were the ones who had approached his client. The judge listened, agreed and threw the case out. When Tene met with reporters later, he assumed a Job-like countenance. "Trouble, trouble and more trouble," he said wearily, "that's all I get from Nichols and his people." A spokesman for the state's attorney snapped, "No comment," but Nichols shortly afterward got out of the *ofisa* business.

Having reasserted his rule over local gypsies, King Tene nonetheless decided that the irate *gadjo* law-enforcement establishment, stung by this latest humiliation, might retaliate in some unknown manner, and he thought it prudent to vacate Chicago for a while. He chose to settle in New York, a city which he had passed through now and then but had never stayed in for any length of time. The most prominent figure in the large Romany community there was Steve Kaslov, the self-proclaimed "King and Judge of All Russian Gypsies in America," a man of guile rather than of action, who resembled the kind of "yassuh" Negro leaders prevalent before black militancy came to the fore.

Tene took up quarters at 139 Park Row, a stone's throw from City Hall in Lower Manhattan, and had been in residence barely a month before he made his move against Kaslov. At about 12:30 A.M. on January 18, 1932, his daughter Rose Bimbo, then using the name McGinnis, showed up crying uncontrollably at a nearby police station with another Bimbo female named Margareta, who was bleeding from a scalp wound. According to a complaint filed by Rose in between sobs, Steve Kaslov, along with three men she did not recognize, had entered the premises at 139 Park Row an hour earlier when she and Margareta were there alone. Two of the men stationed themselves by the front door while Kaslov and the fourth man advanced toward her and Margareta. Kaslov, Rose swore, took out a revolver and said, "Where's the money?" When he did not get an answer, Kaslov struck Margareta once and then again on her head with the gun. After the second blow, Rose continued, Margareta pointed to a locked trunk. Kaslov and one of the other men, upon being told that neither woman had a key to the trunk, broke open the lock with an ax and helped themselves to ten one-hundred-dollar bills. Not being content with this, Rose further deposed, Kaslov at pistol point removed a necklace she was sporting that consisted of fifteen twenty-dollar gold pieces.

Steve Kaslov was arrested the same night in his apartment at 211 East Third Street, arraigned in the morning for robbery and held in bail of five thousand dollars, which was supplied by a bondsman New York gypsies habitually used named Louis Berger. On February 3 Kaslov was indicted by a grand jury for robbery in the first degree, assault in the first degree, grand larceny in the first degree and criminally receiving stolen property. If convicted on all counts, Kaslov, then forty-three, could look forward to spending most of his remaining years in jail.

The case went to trial on March 28. King Tene, as a prosecution witness, played a minor role. He said that he had been at 139 Park Row on the night in question until about ten o'clock, when he and other members of his clan departed to visit a sick friend, leaving Rose and Margareta alone. Queen Mary, however, went on at great length. The thousand dollars taken from the trunk belonged to her. Three years before, she explained, her son Stāvo Bimbo had withdrawn $3,526.22 from a bank and had given her thirty-five hundred, which she carefully husbanded as any good wife would, doling it out from time to time for one emergency or another to keep her family fed, clothed, housed and in good health. She knew, she said, that there was exactly a thousand dollars in the trunk because the very day of the robbery she had counted the money, found it to be one thousand and fifty and took a fifty-dollar bill from the cache to pay the landlord for the coming month's rent. Stāvo Bimbo then took the stand to corroborate his mother's testimony about giving her the money. Rose and Margareta reiterated the statements made in the original complaint. Two police officers attested to the fact that they had inspected the trunk in question and found the lock broken, and an intern on ambulance duty said that Margareta had required medical aid for a cut on her scalp. In the way of physical evidence, no gun or cash had been turned up in Kaslov's apartment, but a pawn ticket for a gold necklace was discovered, although it was dated the day before the crime was supposed to have occurred.

King Steve Kaslov spoke in his own defense, claiming that it was all a frame-up. It was a well-known fact, he said, that "the Bimbo tribe have been framing people and accusing them of various crimes which they never committed, in many cities throughout this country." He added, with evident bitterness, that "Tene Bimbo has been extorting money from gypsies for many years" and that it was because of Kaslov's insistence that "Tene Bimbo and his family stop hounding the New York gypsies and taking money from them under different threats that this charge has been framed by the Bimbo family against me." As an alibi he swore that during the time he was accused of robbing the Bimbos he had been in a restaurant owned by one Frank Stravelli in the Little Italy section of the city. Mr. Stravelli and his wife appeared on Kaslov's behalf and said that they believed this to be true, although under cross-examination they conceded that he had been a steady and valued customer for a number of years. The jury was out for forty-five minutes and found Kaslov guilty on the armed-robbery charge. He was subsequently sentenced to not less than fifteen and not more than twenty-one years in the state penitentiary at Ossining, better known as Sing Sing. Just prior to sentencing, Kaslov's attorney, pleading new evidence, introduced a motion for another trial, but the judge refused, noting, "On the record, your man is no angel."

The new evidence, at best suspect, consisted of depositions from various gypsies certifying that for one reason or another Steve Kaslov could not possibly be guilty of the robbery and that they had not stepped forward during the trial because of their uniform fear of Tene Bimbo. But King Tene's triumph over his rival did not last long. The trial had received widespread publicity, and as a result his past began to catch up with him. The first to contact Kaslov's lawyer was an attorney in Chicago who had represented Angelo Nichols at one point during his losing struggle with Tene. The state's attorney there also was delighted to chime in with a long, uncomplimentary account of Tene Bimbo's activities. And armed with these and other documents, Kaslov's lawyer appealed his conviction. The Chicago Crime Commission, for example, wrote about the Bimbos, "From reports [in our files] it appears that this band of gypsies is constantly in conflict with the law either as complainants or defendants. It is said that this group of gypsies in an attempt to extort money from rival tribes prefers criminal charges against the rival tribes and later approaches them with the proposition of settling for a certain sum of money. If their proposition is not accepted, they proceed against their rivals with the preferred charges." The executive director of the Juvenile Protective Association of Chicago, who had experienced more than one encounter with the Bimbos in general and Rose in particular, declared, "I suppose there has been no gypsy family in Chicago, or in the United States, that has brought such disrepute on the gypsy race as the Bimbos, and Rosie at a very early age began to be of great assistance to her father in the methods he uses. . . . Our records, and all our associations with Rosie and her family, indicate that they are utterly unreliable in their statements." A waiter who was working at the Stravelli restaurant the night of the robbery but who had quit before the trial began was finally located and swore that Kaslov had been there all the time. Additional depositions from gypsies were produced. Some attested to similar past acts by Tene Bimbo; others stated that Margareta had been overheard saying that it was in fact a Bimbo who struck her on the head to make it look as if she had been attacked; still others spoke of threats by Tene to the New York gypsies if they tried to help Kaslov. And while they were often too pat, many of them using the same words to describe an incident, their sheer volume was impressive.

But the most telling documents in the appeal were ones which showed that both Stāvo Bimbo and his sister Rose had lied in their testimony. Before the trial began, Kaslov's lawyer had heard rumors about the Bimbos, especially in Chicago, and had asked the Chicago Police Department for any records it might have on them. He received a reply that all available information had already been passed on to the New York Police Department. But when he pressed his inquiry in New York through a subpoena, he was told that the department had nothing on the Bimbos involved in the case other than one arrest of Rose which had been dismissed—and thus could not be used in the trial. Whether anything had ever been forwarded or had somehow been misplaced was never established. In any event, while Stāvo and Rose Bimbo were on the stand, Kaslov's lawyer, trying a long shot, had asked each of them if they had been previously convicted of a crime, and both had emphatically denied it. At the time, the lawyer had been unable to challenge them. But now, because of all the new documentation he had gathered, he could show that Rose had served time on a pickpocket arrest and that Stāvo Bimbo once pleaded guilty to assault with a deadly weapon.

Almost a year later, on February 15, 1933, the Appellate Division of the New York State Supreme Court reversed Kaslov's conviction, declaring, "If the jury had been aware of the criminal activities and records of the Bimbo family, members of which were the complainants who gave the evidence upon which the defendant was convicted, a verdict of guilty would probably not have been rendered. . . . These records show their malodorous careers of crime, embracing among others extortion, assault and particularly the repeated misuse of the criminal courts by making false accusations against individuals who had incurred their enmity and whose arrest they sought and obtained."

King Tene did achieve a small measure of satisfaction in the end. His rival, King Kaslov, who was not above skulduggery of his own, waited a couple of months and then retaliated by arranging to have a man, listing his occupation as a baker, charge Rose and Margareta with hoodwinking him out of nine hundred dollars in a *boojo* swindle. Tene Bimbo was in court when the two women were arraigned, and afterward he ran into, seemingly by chance, Kaslov's favorite bail bondsman, Louis Berger. Berger, who had had quite a checkered career himself, including the receipt of stolen goods as well as assault and battery, suggested to Tene that for a price—namely, five hundred dollars—he would be able to fix things. Enraged to find himself the target of a shakedown, presumably engineered by Kaslov, Tene pretended to go along with Berger. A down payment of three hundred and fifty dollars was made, and a meeting for the second and final installment was set in a hotel on Manhattan's Lower East Side. Tene Bimbo then told the whole story to the police—using, according to the Bimbos, the alias "Pete Stokes" because of the ill repute that had befallen the clan's name in New York law-enforcement circles. The cops marked the money, listened to the transaction from an adjoining room in the hotel and arrested Berger. The day he was to appear in court, however, the bondsman was discovered dead in a chair in his kitchen, asphyxiated by gas escaping from a stove. There was no note,

and the police theorized that Berger had lighted the
stove to heat a pot of water, had meanwhile fallen
asleep and that the water had boiled over, extinguish-
ing the flame. But there is not a Bimbo around able
to recall the event who doesn't believe that Louis
Berger committed suicide as a result of crossing King
Tene.

Despite this, there was no doubt that Tene had
failed to take over in New York as he had in Chicago,
and after a few months he retired, seething, to Boston
to plan new ventures. His mood was not improved
when his daughter Rose remained in New York and, to
the old man's further annoyance, took up with a
gadjo businessman—a "sugar daddy"—named Charles
Fiske. While the Bimbos were in Boston, Queen Mary
took ill, and Rose, with Fiske in tow, showed up to
visit her. At first Fiske was unwilling to enter Tene's
house in Boston's South End, but he was reassured by
two Bimbo tribesmen that, as he would later testify,
"everything was patched up." He stepped inside with
Rose, who, after visiting with her mother, departed
to do some shopping for her. And for whatever reason,
possibly because of the frustrated rage churning inside
of him, Tene Bimbo suddenly went wild and clubbed
Fiske over the head. When Fiske came to, blood all
over his face, he found himself tied to a chair. According to one of the Bimbos who was in the house at
the time, Tene said to Fiske, "Do you know who I
am?" and Fiske replied, "Yes, Bimbo, I know who
you are," and Tene said, "When you address me, you
call me *Mister* Bimbo," and smashed him in the
mouth with his fist. Then he went to work on Fiske's
body with a pair of pliers. The Bimbo who was there

recalls, "It was terrible, horrible, all them screams. We never saw the old man like that, and all of us was hiding."

Even the hardhearted Rose fainted when she saw what Fiske looked like when she returned. Rose released Fiske, who first had himself treated by a doctor and next pressed charges against Tene, accusing him not only of the assault but also of robbing him of a hundred dollars. Tene was arrested, held in bond of five thousand dollars and because of the ferocity of the attack examined by two court-appointed psychiatrists. In their report, the psychiatrists noted that the prisoner had told them he had suffered a head injury in 1910, had been hospitalized for two weeks and had made a "good" recovery. He denied any other serious injuries and said his general health had always been excellent. He told the doctors that he had never attended school and had been a "member of a nomadic gypsy band until the age of seventeen." He added that after leaving the gypsy band he had "engaged in horse trading with considerable financial success until 1923" and since then had "engaged in the business of being a coppersmith." Tene admitted to three previous arrests in Chicago but said that he had been framed. Under social adaptability the psychiatrists wrote, "Has few interests outside his family and his business. Is a good mixer and socially inclined." They concluded, "While the prisoner is illiterate, he is of at least average normal intelligence. Mentally he shows nothing suggestive of delusions, hallucinations or other abnormal trends. In our opinion the prisoner is not insane and not feeble-minded."

King Tene was indicted by a Boston grand jury and

was about to go on trial when Fiske suddenly declined
to testify against him, either because of fear of what
else Tene might have in store for him, which is what
most Bimbos think, or because of the wiles of Rose,
who might have talked him out of it—or perhaps a
combination of the two. At any rate, Fiske stubbornly
stuck to his new story. He said that he had claimed
Tene had tied him up and had made the other allega-
tions just to "get even with him" and refused to elaborate further.

If his tangling with Steve Kaslov could be considered something of a reversal, Tene Bimbo's fortunes
had turned completely sour by 1936. He was behind
bars for the first extended period in his life—in a
federal penitentiary at Lorton, Virginia. In his early
days King Tene had conducted a thriving little racket
of his own which he continued to indulge in now and
then, although it had become more of a hobby than
anything else, a pastime to amuse himself and to keep
his hand in, as it were.

The hobby was shortchanging banks. Always well
turned out in a suit and vest, Tene would go into a
bank and present a large-denomination bill, one of five
hundred or a thousand dollars, that he wanted to have
changed. He would usually start off by requesting, say,
ten one-hundred-dollar bills. Just as the teller was
counting them out, Tene would come up with a new
request. He had decided that he now wanted five hundred in hundreds, three hundred in fifties and two
hundred in twenties. The teller would begin all over
again, and there would be another interruption. "Make
one of those hundreds tens," Tene would say, "and

one of the twenties fives." He would choose a busy hour, and soon there would be a long line of restless customers behind him which would further rattle the teller. King Tene, however, steadfastly ignored them as he recounted the money being passed to him, palming some of it each time before changing his mind again, sometimes even abruptly asking for five or ten dollars in silver, and often he would mumble his requests in exaggerated broken English so that the teller, on top of all his other problems, would be additionally distracted by having to lean over to hear what Tene was saying.

If an exceptionally fast-counting teller was on the job and caught the shortage before he had left, Tene would resort to the old gypsy trick of dropping the money on the floor and claim that it must have fallen off the counter. But as a rule, the loss was not discovered till the end of the day, at which point an unlucky teller would suddenly remember the portly gentleman with the flowing black mustache who had some trouble making himself understood. Legends sprang up about him. Even among law-enforcement officials the word was that his average take was five hundred dollars. But in fact he was far more modest in his aims. A profit of a hundred and fifty was all he actually expected to realize in a thousand-dollar-bill transaction, and no more than fifty or seventy-five from one of five hundred dollars.

The laws of chance finally caught up with him in Washington, D.C. He was nabbed stealing a hundred and fifty from one bank, although he claimed that the money was his to begin with, and then it was discovered that his description fit that of a man involved in a similar theft the same day in another Washington bank for a hundred and thirty. Worse yet, while he was being held for questioning, Tene turned out to be wanted in a score of other cities for the identical con, and he wound up being sentenced to a two-to-eight-year term in the Lorton prison.

While King Tene was serving time, a second disaster struck the Bimbo tribe. Queen Mary, who had returned to Chicago, was arrested on April 26, 1937, for swindling a Wisconsin farmer named Stanley Kozak in a *boojo*. Earlier that month, according to Kozak, he, his wife and his daughter had visited Chicago, where they passed a fortune-telling establishment. They went in and had their futures predicted by a gypsy woman later identified by Kozak as Queen Mary. During his session with her, Kozak revealed to Queen Mary that he was not feeling as well as he might, and she instructed him to return alone later in the day. He did, and Queen Mary confided that he was "very lucky" to have come to her, since the twinges he had been experiencing were early-warning signs of a terminal illness caused by some "evil" hanging over him. On two successive visits Kozak was dazzled by the devil's-head-in-the-egg and the boiling water routines as evidence of his precarious condition. Then Queen Mary told Kozak that she had received a "message." All his ills were being caused by cursed money; he was to bring her at least a thousand dollars to be exorcised, along with a live rooster. She would, she said, try to transfer the evil threatening Kozak to the rooster. The obedient Kozak purchased a rooster, as he testified, for $1.05 and also brought along all the cash he could scrape up—six hundred dollars. Queen Mary grumbled a bit at the amount but said she would do her best. She took the money, wrapped it in a handkerchief and appeared to pin the same handkerchief to Kozak's shirt over his heart. She then held the rooster next to the handkerchief and informed Kozak that the moment of truth had arrived. If everything went well, the rooster would absorb the evil caused by the money and die, and Kozak would live. As for the alternative, Queen Mary simply shrugged. She began to pray, moving the rooster around the handkerchief pinned to Kozak's chest, and all at once there was a brief flutter and the rooster was dead. Kozak vividly recalled how one of the rooster's spurs scraped across his throat before it died. He was ordered to tell nobody what had taken place and to keep the handkerchief with him, unopened, for nine days, by which time Queen Mary planned to be in New York. But before she could get away, Kozak forgot to take the handkerchief with him one morning; his wife found it under his pillow and unfolded it and asked her husband what he was doing with a handkerchief full of blank paper, and he shamefacedly went to the police.

From prison King Tene sent word to Queen Mary to delay her trial as long as possible in the hope that he would be paroled in time to mastermind her defense. She posted a five-thousand-dollar bond and won several continuances by switching lawyers, but finally, when Tene's bid to get out was refused in the fall of 1937, she had no choice except to jump bail, something she had successfully done before in three other cases. This time, however, she was located in New York and was returned to Chicago. On March 1, 1938, she made one last stab at another continuance on the grounds that the lawyer she had retained had not shown up in court, but the judge appointed a public defender to represent her. She waived a jury trial and was found guilty and sentenced to one to ten years at the State Reformatory for Women at Dwight, Illinois. The following October the State Supreme Court affirmed her conviction. She had appealed on the grounds that she had been forced to use a public defender against her will, and he in turn had talked her out of a trial by jury, which was what she really wanted. The court, noting that she had obtained twelve continuances using four different attorneys, dismissed the public-defender issue at once; it also said that on the record she fully understood what she was doing when she waived a jury trial and added that the evidence was overwhelming that she had obtained the money "by means of a confidence game."

Queen Mary got more crushing news when she became eligible for parole after a year in the reformatory. The Illinois Pardon and Parole Board ruled that she would have to serve the normal maximum period for this type of sentence—a total of six years and three months. The board's decision was heavily influenced by a psychiatric examination of Queen Mary which described her in part as an "obese gypsy who has a friendly manner, smiles readily, but admits nothing," and further noted that "she lies with a perfectly straight face and projects all her blame onto others." In recommending no parole, the report concluded, "Prognosis for good social adjustment by this prisoner is very poor in view not only of her long antisocial record but also of her failure to accept any blame for it."

By then King Tene had been released from Lorton

and was allowed to rejoin his family in Chicago, where he had to report regularly to a probation officer. Conference after conference was held among the Bimbos about Queen Mary's plight. Since every legal means had been exhausted, she had to be freed some other way, but how? While the reformatory was not anything like a maximum-security facility, it was still a prison, and one did not walk in and out at will. Nonetheless Tene went there to see her and to look the place over. Queen Mary spoke bitterly to him about the denial of her own parole and also mentioned the "crazy" tests she had undergone, and by the time he was back in Chicago he had an idea which would lead to a classic prison escape.

Bimbos traveled to Dwight on every visiting day, and through them King Tene sent word to her to "act crazy" and to keep it up. He did not know exactly where this would lead but figured that it was at least a first step in possibly getting her into some kind of hospital where he could make his next move. He purposely never saw her again while she was in custody because he had to worry about his probation officer and wanted to make sure that no one could connect him directly to what he had in mind.

The change in Queen Mary's behavior at the reformatory was noticed almost immediately. One report expressed some perplexity: "It is difficult to determine the extent of this woman's retardation." Another declared, "She introduces fantasy very freely into her stories, but there is no evidence of psychosis." A third comment raised the possibility of a transfer: "If further psychological tests show definite retardation, advisability of commitment to an institution for the feeble-minded might be considered."

The Bimbos waited impatiently for something to happen, and then they got a lucky break. On October 1, 1939, Queen Mary's best friend at the reformatory, another inmate named Christine Sedirvy, died. Queen Mary was kept under observation to see what ill effects the death might have on her, and she seized the opportunity to go into a precipitous decline. "She is disoriented from place, does not recognize personnel and does not respond to questions regarding orientation or time," a new analysis disclosed. "She is experiencing visual and auditory hallucinations and must be watched closely for possible suicidal attempt. This patient is acutely psychotic, and sedatives and hydrotherapy are indicated. If she continues to be disturbed, a transfer to the Kankakee State Hospital is recommended."

It was the most important con she had ever engaged in, and Queen Mary played it to the hilt. Supervisory personnel observed her running around swatting at invisible targets. When she was asked what she was doing, she said, "Don't you see them? I'm killing them. I'm killing the rats!" Then one day she was found sitting in a chair rocking an object wrapped in a towel, crooning softly. She was asked again what she was doing, and she replied, "I'm taking care of the baby. The baby's sick." The towel was unfolded and was found to contain a roll of toilet paper.

That seemed to do it. On October 6 she was certified insane and transferred to the Kankakee State Hospital, a mental-health facility situated about sixty-five miles south of Chicago. Most of the patients then were wards of the court. Only a small percentage had come from correctional institutions; and like Queen Mary, they were there for rehabilitation under an agreement with the prison administration that they would be returned once their condition had improved. Those patients who had been judged criminally insane and dangerous, which was not the case with her, were isolated in a closed ward and were not permitted any unsupervised freedom of movement. Otherwise, even patients who had been jailed had the same privileges as any others there and could stroll around the grounds and live in "open wards" that consisted of two-story limestone and sandstone buildings, somewhat like old country mansions. On the top floor of each was a long room, about three hundred by one hundred feet with row upon row of beds, occasionally broken by small partitions, which could house as many as a hundred and eighty inmates. The ground floor was for recreation and visitors, divided into four rooms with several sitting arrangements composed of a sofa, a table and some chairs, and the basement contained a cafeteria and a kitchen.

In addition to the hospital personnel there were about twenty guards. Visiting passes were picked up at the administration building. The names of all visitors were registered, and a visiting pass was issued. Normally, with this pass, only two visitors could actually see a particular patient at one time, while the others waited their turn. But as King Tene initiated the next phase of his plan, Bimbos by the droves came from Chicago and elsewhere to spend time with her, blithely ignoring the two-visitors-to-a-pass regulation, some pretending not to understand English, cajoling the guards, the younger girls flirting with them, others providing a constant stream of pleasantries, promising to tell their fortunes, crying out gaily, "We're here to see our mother!" or "We're here to see our Queen!" At first there was some resistance on the part of the hospital security forces, but gradually they got used to the flood of gypsies who descended upon them and began to view their arrival with resigned amusement.

Early in the afternoon on March 18, 1940, twelve Bimbos—four men and eight women—came to see Queen Mary. The women, as usual, were dressed in blouses and swirling skirts, their heads wrapped in bandanas. One of them was wearing a second skirt, another had on an extra blouse, a third had tucked away another kerchief, and as they huddled excitedly around her, Queen Mary quickly exchanged her hospital clothes for the new garments and shortly thereafter walked out in their midst, laughing and chattering away. Just to make certain that the attention of the last guard they had to pass was diverted, a Bimbo tribesman gave him a twenty-dollar tip, asking that he look after the gypsy lady.

The original plan was to have one of the Bimbo females sneak upstairs and get into Queen Mary's bed, pull the covers over her head, stay there until she was discovered and then claim that she had simply decided to take a nap and had no idea what all the ruckus was about. But Queen Mary informed her rescuers that there really was no need to put anyone in possible jeopardy, since the hospital had grown lax about counting heads at supper and the only check they had to worry about was at bedtime, still several hours off.

The Bimbos, together with Queen Mary, departed in two cars. Nobody felt any exhilaration at that point. "We feared," one of them involved in the great escape said. "We feared that any second we would be hearing the sirens and we would be caught and would lose her again." She was given another change of clothing, and after traveling approximately ten miles, the two cars stopped and she was transferred to a third car parked by the roadside. The third car headed east toward the Indiana border, while the two cars with the Bimbos who had registered at the hospital sped back to Chicago. In the car now carrying Queen Mary, two Bimbo women went to work dying her hair red and applying cosmetics. "You never would of recognized her," I was told. "She looked ten, fifteen years younger." The only problem was with Queen Mary herself, who grumbled continually about not being allowed to savor her pipe.

Short of the Indiana line she was moved to a fourth car and eventually spent what was left of the night in a Detroit hotel. She was then driven to New York, where for about a year she stayed in an apartment in East Harlem. The wanted bulletin on her read: "Mary Bimbo, also known as Mary Tene, Mary Pulitch, Margaret Puloch and Margaretta Polish. Female gypsy, age 51, five feet, six inches tall, about 171 pounds, black hair, brown eyes, swarthy complexion, conjugal. Well-known operator of all types of gypsy swindles. Usually accompanied by various members of her family." A mug shot, showing her grinning broadly, was also distributed.

But she was never found.

Around ten o'clock in the evening on the day of her escape, as the Bimbos expected, the police arrived at two residences they were known to have in Chicago, one on South Halsted Street and the other on Blue Island Avenue. Pretending to have been aroused from a sound sleep, the Bimbos asked the cops what was going on and were told about the missing Queen Mary. They replied that they had last seen her at the hospital a few hours before, when she had waved a cheery good-bye. It remained for King Tene to take the lead. He suddenly began railing at the police, demanding to know what had happened to his wife, threatening to sue the city and the state. "You took her from us," he screamed. "She was in your hands! What did you do to her?" The cops, taken aback, promised to investigate the matter further.

Tene, who had been forced to remain behind in Chicago because of his parole requirements, kept up his attack against the police, the state prison officials, the hospital administration. He paid particular attention to his probation officer, demanding to know from him how such a thing could have occurred. But slowly, especially with the probation officer, he began to change his tune. Instead of implying that the state had been involved in some sort of nefarious plot against his wife, he slid into wounded despair. "How could they have let her done that?" he would say, bursting into tears, while the probation officer tried to console him. "You know what I'm saying, how could they let her wander off like that? She's maybe laying in a ditch somewhere or in the river without a decent burial or nothing." Finally he brought up the fact that because of all the "bad memories" it had, he couldn't abide staying in Chicago any longer, and he was permitted, a year after the escape, to move to New York.

Once there, his main concern was his old rival, Steve Kaslov, who was then basking in considerable press coverage for getting his followers to attend what turned out to be a short-lived, federally sponsored reading and writing course for gypsies in the city. Tene's worry was that Kaslov might learn of Queen Mary's presence in the New York area and tip off the police. So late one night, together with three armed Bimbo tribesmen, he approached Kaslov in an Italian restaurant at 117 Mott Street in Lower Manhattan. The restaurant was called Puglia, after the Italian province of the same name, and featured regional dishes such as tripe and other animal innards and a variety of ragouts as well as roasted lamb's head, all delicacies that gypsies favor. Kaslov was just leaving when Tene Bimbo arrived, and he was marched at gunpoint into the restaurant's ice room in the rear where perishables were stored. Still covered by a revolver, Kaslov was hoisted onto one of the meat hooks so that it pierced his overcoat and jacket, no small feat, since at the time he weighed in the neighborhood of two hundred pounds. Before it ripped through his clothing and he fell to the floor, King Tene had time to tell him that he was back in New York but would make no attempt to horn in on any of Kaslov's activities. In return he expected that he and his tribe would be left alone. Otherwise, he warned, the next time Kaslov was on a meat hook, it would be in him and not his coat.

The message apparently got through, and Queen

Mary remained around New York until she died on May 17, 1951. At the last moment she was rushed to Gouverneur Hospital as Susie Johnson. The Bimbos wanted her death certificate to read Mary Tene, but the doctor signing it refused any name other than the one she was registered under. In the end, however, they got their way where it counted, and her tombstone at the Hollywood Cemetery in Union, New Jersey, reads "Mary Tene."

After he had arranged Queen Mary's escape, King Tene continued to be embroiled in one gypsy wrangle after another, but he usually managed to stay clear of the law himself, his confrontations with the police and his appearances in court limited to briefs on behalf of various members of his tribe. On one occasion, when some Bimbos had been arrested, he yelled at the cops, "Why you pick on my people all the time? What about the other tribes? How much they paying you off?" Upon being told that if he had information about any such graft, it was his duty as an American citizen to report it, he replied, "Fuck America. I ain't no stool pigeon." And even late in his life, he remained as intractable as ever. At the age of seventy-five, when a New York newspaper, the *Daily Mirror,* ran a series on gypsies which in the first article featured photographs of some Bimbos, he promptly invaded the paper's offices together with about thirty of his tribesmen and raised such a furor that the editors, while continuing the series, agreed to stop printing any more Bimbo pictures.

Now, in 1969, in Park East Hospital, where it all would end, King Tene still put up a battle. From the time he went in on October 14 his condition steadily improved for three days. He alone among all the gypsies at the hospital seemed prepared to face the reality of his situation, and it was on the seventeenth that he dropped the bombshell that he wanted his most precious, symbolic possessions to go to his grandson, Steve Tene. "I wish for young Stevie," he said, "to have the ring and the medallion so he can make something of himself."

As one of the Bimbos who was present told me, "We didn't, nobody did, say anything about it at that time. Because then all we was doing was thinking about the old man. We didn't think he was going to die, you know, and we thought we could question the point with him when he comes out of his sickness." But on the eighteenth he started to decline. "Patient was then in heart failure," his summary medical report read. For the next three days he went up and down, hanging on, but losing strength after each crisis. On October 22 he appeared even weaker. He had a temperature for the first time and was on intravenous medication, and while his lungs were clear, he complained of feeling cold in his hands and feet. "At 1:40 in the afternoon," the medical report continued, "the patient expired suddenly."

One of his last requests was that both the American and Russian flags be flown at his funeral. The latter provoked considerable debate until one elder observed, "All our tribe will be cursed if we don't honor his wishes." A Soviet flag was obtained easily enough from the Russian consulate, but then the thought occurred to everybody that something untoward might happen in a cortege featuring a flag with the hammer and sickle on it. So a delegation of Bimbos went to City Hall to ask for a police escort, which they got. Mayor John Lindsay also sent a telegram expressing his condolences. This infuriated the Bimbos, who felt that the mayor should have shown up in person.

As a local television reporter who covered the event recalled, "It wasn't your usual, run-of-the-mill funeral." The wake, held at the Walter B. Cooke Funeral Home at Eighty-fifth Street and Third Avenue, lasted three days and three nights. To handle the crowd, the Cooke home opened up first one, then two of its biggest rooms on the ground floor. At least a thousand gypsies came in to pay their respects. The bronze coffin, which cost three thousand dollars, was left open, as is the gypsy custom, the corpse covered by a veil of white lace. Visitors thrust money and occasionally a bottle of whiskey into the coffin both to provide expenses to the departed on his journey into the hereafter and to quench his thirst. There were dozens of floral displays, many of them of a gambling nature—a horse's head, an Exacta ticket, a bingo card, a pair of dice with the numbers four and three on them—dominated by a huge symbolic gateway arch of flowers. Although it is against the law, food—turkeys, hams and the like— and drink were passed through the windows of the funeral home, and the assembled gypsies partook of this, chatted, dozed, played cards and generally caught up with one another's doings.

The funeral procession itself was led by bearers of the United States and Soviet flags and an eight-piece band which played such tunes as "God Bless America," "Onward, Christian Soldiers," "When the Saints Go Marching In," "The Battle Hymn of the Republic" and "So Long, It's Been Good to Know Yuh." The cortege created a memorable traffic jam as it solemnly made its way downtown to the Cathedral of the Holy Virgin, a Russian Orthodox church on the Lower East Side. There was a moment of tension when the officiating prelate objected to the presence of a Communist standard on his altar, but this was resolved by an additional cash contribution to worthy charities in the name of the dead king.

After the service a motorcade followed King Tene's remains to the Hollywood Cemetery in New Jersey, where he was laid to rest alongside Queen Mary and surrounded by other gypsies who had purchased plots there. The coffin was opened one last time and more money—bills and gold coins—thrown into it, together with some liquor and wine, and it was then, when the old man's face was covered for good and his body lowered into the grave, that the weeping and cries of grief began.

In trying to keep tabs on the gypsies, the New York Police Department maintains charts full of circles and squares and arrows on the various tribes and their relationships, much as they do with Mafia families. It is enough to make the successive custodians of these diagrams certifiably committable. And to cope with the maze of Romany name changes and constant movement, the department depends to a large extent on photographs to determine who's who and who's where. So an occasion like King Tene Bimbo's death had Detective Eddie Coyne, along with a partner, on duty busily snapping pictures. When his partner expressed astonishment at the crowd that had turned out, Coyne said, "They're not here to honor him. They just want to make sure he's dead."

PART
IV

***

The Circle

Steve Tene had already left the gypsy life and was in Los Angeles when his grandfather died. As a boy, however, he had always had a special rapport with the old man, and he was preparing to go to the funeral when an uncle, Adolph Bimbo, called him. "Don't show up," the uncle said, "or I'll have you shot."

"It was because of Stevie and his father," one of King Tene Bimbo's daughters told me. "There was all that trouble between them and we don't want no trouble at the funeral, you know what I mean?"

The mourning period for the old man, as is usual after gypsy deaths, lasted twelve months, interspersed with a feast in his honor six weeks after his demise and another near the end of the year. On these occasions clothes are given to close friends of the departed on his behalf, and in Tene's case they went to two old drinking companions in New York, a Spanish gypsy named Stefano and a Russian gypsy known as "The Colonel." "They were just social friends," the daughter said. "He never done no business with them, so it was right and proper that they should get the clothes. They were bought at the best store. I think it was Rogers Peet."

When this mourning period was over, Steve received his grandfather's medallion and the ring. They simply arrived in the mail. Since there was such hostility toward him as a renegade, I suggested to the daughter that it would have been relatively easy to forget about the legacy. A horrified look crossed her face. "We could not dishonor my father's wishes," she exclaimed. "Nobody would dare do that!" Yet like every gypsy of any seniority that I met, she was appalled by the legacy itself and groped for some kind of rationalization. "My father was a leader," the daughter said, "and maybe he saw some of what he was in Stevie. Times were changing, and maybe the old ways weren't so good any more, and his own sons were too old and set in their life to do anything about it. My father, you know, did things that were not in our tradition in his own time. When he was still a young man and one of our people was sick, he would say, 'We cannot help him with our prayers and our leaves and roots. We got to take him to the *gadjo* hospital.' And he would talk to the doctors himself and arrange everything, like he did with the sheriff and the police when one of our people was in jail. He was feared, you know, he was a killer, but he was wise too, and there was something between him and Stevie, and Stevie would talk to him about how we got to Americanize ourselves and not be different no more. And at each holiday, Christmas and Easter and feasts like that, after Stevie had run away, the old man always had his name on his lips at the table and he'd say put aside some food for Stevie 'cause he might show up."

When Steve as a kid had fled from his father and was surviving in New York as a male prostitute, and then was found by members of the Bimbo tribe standing in a doorway on Forty-second Street, he was brought first to his grandfather. Several days passed before King Tene referred to his long absence and the circumstances under which he had been found. "What you did was a terrible thing," he observed at last, "but you're going back to your father now, and everything will be all right."

Steve could not bring himself to tell his grandfather the reason he had fled the apartment in Philadelphia, how the father had tried to force him into bed with his mother. Instead he started to cry. "I'm not going back to Carranza," he sobbed. "You don't know what happened! I went through everything on account of him. I took dope. I had to hustle men. Ain't it enough I had that fucking life on the streets?"

But the old man put it on a personal basis, and Steve could not refuse him. "Do this favor for *me*," King Tene Bimbo said, "not your father. I spoke to him and he gave me his word he won't touch you. So go to him and be a good son, and you'll find a nice surprise."

The surprise was a wife purchased for Steve by his father on orders of the grandfather. Her name was Dina. She was a pretty girl with chestnut hair who was five years older than Steve and came from the Demetro tribe, another important clan of Kalderash gypsies. She was supposed to be a virgin, and after their first night together he watched, fascinated, as she nicked a vein in her wrist and put blood on the sheet. "It's our secret," she told him. "The other time don't matter."

Steve's mother examined the sheet, and he was certain she knew what had happened. But she apparently chose not to voice her suspicions to his father out of fear of what he might do.

In the end it did not make any difference. Carranza behaved reasonably well for about a month after the wedding until without warning one morning all the latent cruelty in him exploded again. His new daughter-in-law was making his breakfast. He liked his fried eggs turned over, and as she was preparing them, one of the yolks broke. She made the mistake of serving him the egg with the broken yolk, and he began cursing her, the crescendo of obscenities steadily mounting. Suddenly he spat in the eggs, sending a huge wad of phlegm into them, and screamed at the girl, "Sit down! *You* eat them."

There was a time when Steve's father had been a slim, almost elegantly handsome man, but he had become a gross, balding, surly-faced, bullnecked figure full of menace, with a powerful torso still discernible under the fat that had accumulated during years of dissipation, given to walking around sockless day and night, a sports shirt flopping over his fifty-odd-inch girth. The terrified girl did as she was told, and immediately fell subject to the gypsy code of *marimay*. She had been made unclean. She could no longer take her meals at the same table with the rest of the family, had to keep her own plate, glass and eating utensils apart from the others and became virtually untouchable not only in the house of her in-laws but in the residence of any gypsy she happened to be visiting.

When Steve learned what had occurred, it meant the end of his marriage. "I couldn't sleep with her any more," he told me. "I couldn't take the chance, like if we had a kid he might turn out to be blind or dumb or something because my father had wished it on her, on us."

I asked him how he, allegedly so emancipated, could go along with such nonsense, and he said, "It isn't nonsense. I don't know why it is, but a spell like my father did, it gets into a girl's head. Psychologically the girl puts it in her own head, she believes it, and she does end up no good. That's a fact. Maybe it's not in the girl really, but she's like brainwashed and she thinks she's that way even if she isn't."

He went to his grandfather for help, but King Tene refused to intervene. "You got to work this out with your father yourself," he said. Steve's wife stood the strain for perhaps two weeks and then disappeared. He made no attempt to find her. "If you want the truth," he said, "I felt sorry for her, and I figured she was better off starting a new life somewhere. I didn't love her. I hardly knew her. Gypsy marriages ain't supposed to be happy. You're supposed to struggle together to make a life and fall in love afterwards."

A few days later Steve himself ran away again, although this time he stayed generally within the gypsy life, shuttling back and forth across the country, joining first one Romany band and then another. He was older now and he had little trouble finding acceptance because he was an expert driver and, unlike most male gypsies, did not mind working. For the better part of five years he drove for girls as they ripped off neighborhood after neighborhood, made accident cases with them in supermarkets, movie theaters and department stores, and chauffeured *boojo* women to *ofisas* from

Miami to Seattle, Boston to Los Angeles for a percentage of their profits.

After a *boojo* woman had rented a store, Steve would help carry in the folding chairs and tables, sleeping bags, quilts and a portable stove and would hang all the drapes to partition the *ofisa*. Afterward he would pass out handbills announcing "Sister Annie" or "Mrs. Reed" or "Mother Sophia" was in town and ready to aid troubled souls. These handbills, often decorated with art work featuring Jesus the Good Shepherd or the Virgin and Child, provided precise public-transit instructions such as "Bus #42 leaves you at her door." No personal distress was too much for a *boojo* woman to tackle. Sister Annie's ad, for example, proclaimed, "Help on all problems. If sick, worried or in difficulties, she will help you. If you lost the one you love, or have no peace of mind, come to her for help." Mother Sophia seemed to have the same copywriter. "No matter how difficult your problem may be she'll lift you from your burden," her handbill read. "Advice on all problems of life such as love, courtship, marriage, divorce, separation, health, financial difficulties. If sick, worried, if life is passing you by, don't fail to see her today. There's no pity for those in need of help who don't help themselves." Mrs. Reed's flyer struck a more positive note: "She'll tell you what you want to know about your friends, enemies or rivals, whether your husband, wife or sweetheart is true or false, how to gain the love you most desire and how to rid yourself of evil influence and bad spells." As a special inducement "this week only" she also offered blessed oil and candles free with each reading.

When Steve drove gypsy girls around residential

areas looking for likely victims to rob, they got into apartments or houses mostly by using the device of delivering a vial of holy water to some sick person whose address they claimed they had lost. But now and then the girls would try to sell what they said were "magic flowers" for a quarter or fifty cents as a means of gaining entry. They are actually called Jericho flowers or resurrection plants and were first discovered near the Red Sea. In their dormant state they seem to be nothing more than dead, brownish clumps of curled leaves with dried roots equally lifeless in appearance, but when placed in water, their leaves slowly uncurl and turn a vibrant green. If you owned one, the girls said, any problems you had would change for the better in the same miraculous manner, especially, they added with a wink, those of a sexual nature.

On occasion Steve encountered another gypsy boy willing to exert himself, and they would go "blacktopping" together. They would cruise around in a panel truck looking for driveways that needed repair. When they found one, they would approach the homeowner and say that while they were regularly employed by a resurfacing company, they didn't mind making a little extra money on the side, and they would propose to do the driveway at half the going rate. Whoever snapped up the offer was left with a glistening new surface of crankcase oil and paint thinner that vanished following the first rainfall.

During this period Steve returned to his family three times. About six months after he had left because of the *marimay* visited upon his wife, he was brought back forcibly by one of his father's brothers. The next time was when Carranza was supposedly on his deathbed in a Columbus, Ohio, hospital. He came back the third time after his mother had tearfully pleaded with him on the phone that life was unbearable without someone to chauffeur her around on her con game, which she was then practicing in Philadelphia. A week or so after Steve's return, Carranza awoke one morning, hung over, and again went into one of his sudden, unpredictable rages, took out the big .38-caliber revolver with an ivory handle he habitually carried on his travels, pumped two shots into an ancient sofa and announced that the next bullet would be for Steve. His mother intervened and smoothed things over, but Steve left the same morning. After that he managed to stay out of Carranza's path, although once, in New York, he was cornered on Columbus Avenue by Bimbo gypsies close to his father and was savagely beaten.

Except for the violence he personally associated with his father, Steve's vagabond life was otherwise peaceful. He knew, of course, about his grandfather's reputation but none of the details. He also had heard of increasingly violent crimes committed by gypsies. One of his cousins, also named Steve, had been detained in Logan Airport in Boston after an airlines agent became suspicious of a check that he was using to buy a ticket. A Massachusetts state trooper was questioning him when he yanked a gun out of a briefcase and started pulling the trigger at pointblank range. The first two tries misfired, and in the ensuing struggle the gun finally fired but missed the trooper. While being held for trial, the cousin was one of the participants in a dramatic escape attempt from the city jail that was foiled as they were spotted climbing down a forty-foot rope made from sheets, and he ended up with a long prison sentence. There were other examples of changing times. A Bimbo boy, aged seventeen, was apprehended after he had knocked an eighty-five-year-old woman to the ground and run off with her purse containing one hundred and seventy dollars and a diamond ring. Juvenile gypsies also were turning more and more to narcotics—a direct result of the *gadjo* influence on them, the Romany Aunt Hazels would say—and gypsy youths posing as telephone repairmen or light-and-power maintenance crews would get inside a residence and, if necessary, club the occupants to get the money they needed to support their drug habits.

In 1968 this kind of violence caught up with Steve when he arrived in New Orleans with a band of gypsies to fatten on the Mardi Gras crowd. After the celebration had ended—pockets picked and *boojo* swindles completed—a few gypsies stayed on, Steve among them. Late one night he was cruising the streets in a car with three gypsy girls, the oldest eighteen. They spotted a derelict poking through some garbage cans on the sidewalk. To the naked eye he looked like just another bum, but the eighteen-year-old said, "Stop, Stevie, I smell money." She got out and took the derelict's arm as if she were trying to pick him up. He pushed her away, and they started to scuffle. Steve honked his horn, signaling her to stop. "No, no," she yelled, "he's full of money."

The man broke loose and hurried around a corner. The girl, whose name was Lenka, ran back to the car. "I felt his money belt, I'm telling you, he's full of dollars." When Steve turned the corner, the man was boarding a bus. "Follow the bus," Lenka insisted. "We'll get him when he gets off. Oh, my goddamn wrist! That old prick hurt my wrist."

Even Steve found it hard to believe that their bedraggled quarry had any money, but he had seen too many instances of gypsy girls being able to sense cash on the most unlikely people, and when this apparent vagrant finally descended from the bus on the city's outskirts, he knew they were right again. "You'd never dream," he recalled, "that he'd be living in this house with a big fence and a locked gate. You'd have to figure he'd be sleeping in some hallway."

Lenka said to one of the other girls, "Give me that wrench," and all three were out of the car before Steve could do anything to stop them and on top of the man while he was still fumbling with his keys in the darkness. He shouted for help, and then Lenka was swinging the wrench and he went down. Steve started to get out of the car, but the girls by now were on their way back, and lights in a house across the street were being turned on and then another car was coming down the street. So Steve stepped on the gas and raced off, yelling at the girls in the rear seat, "What are you, crazy? That guy could be dead!" The girls, greedily counting the cash in the money belt they had taken, did not answer. Finally Lenka exclaimed, "There's seven, eight thousand dollars here. And *you* wanted us to leave him go?"

Gypsy guile in stealing was one thing, but a brutal attack like this was quite something else, and Steve remained awake all night wondering how seriously injured the old man was, worrying whether somebody had got a description of the car, expecting the police to arrive at any moment. Worst of all, the girls were totally unconcerned about what had happened. Only the money mattered. And in a way, he had gone along with the mugging, had done nothing really to halt it, and he saw himself being sucked into violent acts like this again and again.

He had to get out. He had been bothered anyway by the restiveness of his life. There ought to be some point to it, yet all he seemed to do was to move in circles, just existing, and he thought, where the hell am I going? This unease had been reflected in one of the songs he had composed and memorized, the lyrics describing "a lonely gypsy boy" walking the streets night and day, not knowing what to do and calling upon someone to guide him. And so the morning after the assault on the old man, he left for Los Angeles. He had about a thousand dollars with him, and while he tried to plan what to do next, he rented a room in Hollywood and spent his nights hanging around the clubs on "The Strip." One afternoon he was hitchhiking to Burbank to visit a friend. A couple in their early forties gave him a ride. He learned that they had just bought a house in the San Fernando Valley and that the husband was a technician at one of the big movie studios. Steve at once began asking questions about film-making. Then, when he told them that he was a gypsy, they in turn plied him with more questions. The upshot was that they invited him to stop in for a cup of coffee. He wound up staying for dinner, the visit to his friend forgotten. The couple had two little girls, seven and eleven, whom Steve instantly charmed. The husband showed him around the house, which needed painting, and spoke ruefully about all the furniture that he never seemed to have time to fix.

It was the first evening Steve had spent with a *gadjo*

family at home. He liked what he saw. He suddenly said that he would spackle and paint and refurbish the place in return for room and board. He had always enjoyed working with his hands and remembered with pleasure the brief period he had spent refinishing antiques when he was a runaway in New York. The couple, captivated by his quiet, easygoing manner, took him up on the offer. After he had completed their house, he began to do odd jobs around the neighborhood and then was hired on as a refinisher in an antique store on Melrose Avenue in Los Angeles. He continued to live with the couple, paying them twenty dollars a week, thinking of them as his parents, the only ones he really ever had. He found none of this particularly unusual. For Steve Tene, gypsy, that's how life was. Things just happened, and if they did not pan out, he would just move on.

Within a year he had launched his own refinishing business; he also sold antiques on consignment and had acquired his first Hollywood star, Ricardo Montalban, as a customer. Although he was picking up spare cash in traditional gypsy fashion—buying broken-down automobiles from used-car dealers, doing some minimal repair work and then advertising them as privately owned, tenderly cared-for vehicles and reselling them at a profit—he needed more than that to get the business going and finally financed it with a twenty-five-hundred-dollar settlement from another fake accident case in which he claimed a concussion, impairment of balance and a dislocated disc after tripping on a piece of torn carpet and falling spectacularly down a flight of stairs in a movie theater.

On occasion he saw and socialized with gypsies in the

Los Angeles area, and since little remains a secret in the Romany world for very long, his telephone number became known, and one night a cousin called from New York and told him that his grandfather, King Tene Bimbo, was dead. Steve instantly remembered how he had searched for the old man as a twelve-year-old fleeing Carranza, and he wondered whether his life would have been any different if he had found his grandfather at the end of that walk in the night up Broadway so long ago. When he received the warning not to attend the funeral, he sent twelve dozen red roses, unsigned. Then, almost a year later, the ring and the medallion arrived with a terse note that the grandfather had wanted him to have them. Steve put them in a safe deposit box and continued to immerse himself in his business. But word of King Tene's legacy spread quickly, and younger gypsies began seeking him out, asking him what he proposed to do.

"Nothing."

"But you know what the ring and the medallion mean?"

"No," he would reply sarcastically. "Tell me."

"Your grandfather wants you to follow in his footsteps."

"Well, that's too bad. I'm not interested."

All this changed, however, after a call from his father, then in Chicago, who demanded that he return as a wayward son begging forgiveness for his past transgressions. The usual threats followed, recriminations flew back and forth, and Steve finally hung up on him.

A week later, when Steve's "foster" mother was home alone, a man knocked at the door and claimed he was from the light-and-power company to check the meter.

After he had gone, she stepped into the back yard for a moment. There was an explosion. She rushed into the house and found the kitchen in shambles.

The explosion had originated in the stove, and local fire-department officials first thought that some defect in it had caused the blast. But then traces of dynamite were discovered.

His foster parents, who were aware of what was going on, expressed considerable nervousness about what else might happen, especially with the two girls in the house, and to save them further grief, Steve moved out and rented a cottage in Hermosa Beach along the coast just south of Los Angeles. He felt now that even if he wanted to, he could not duck the issue of his grandfather's will, and his first chance to assert himself occurred among the Bimbos in San Francisco, where he went to visit the oldest of his six sisters, who was seriously ill. Yes, he told them, he had decided to honor the wishes of the tribe's dead leader and would try to carry on for him. But the message he brought was heretical. Gypsies had to become educated. They had to learn to read and write. They had to become law-abiding citizens. They had to shuck their cloistered ways and become part of the community. Where, he demanded, was the gypsy doctor, lawyer, scientist? It might be too late for gypsies their age, but it was not too late for their children. "Do you want them," he said, "to grow up like you and me?"

In America today it is strange to think that what Steve Tene was saying could be considered revolutionary, but for most gypsies that was precisely the case, and for others it sounded like some new con. Not all of them, however, reacted like this. One of Steve's converts is a pretty, twenty-year-old gypsy woman named Lulu, who was twice sold into disastrous Romany marriages and has a seven-year-old daughter. She lives in New York, and after listening to Steve she is sending the daughter to school and has a job on a factory assembly line. Twice a week she attends an adult remedial-reading class. Most of her friends are *gadje,* and on Saturday night, instead of stealing as she once did, she goes bowling. She says that she will not marry again, except for love. If she does, she would prefer that her husband be a gypsy, but he must work. I asked her why she had changed her life style so completely. "We respected Stevie's grandfather," she told me, "and we know what his grandfather gave him, and that he had a reason for this. Stevie is trying to get us civilized."

There are still not many Lulus, but each of these fissures in the age-old Romany social structure sent the gypsy establishment into a frenzy. And one night when Steve was asleep in his Hermosa Beach place, the garage where he kept his pickup truck, his refinishing equipment and the furniture he was working on suddenly caught fire. He was insured, but ironically, because of the suspicious nature of the blaze, he had more trouble collecting the money than in any of his phony accident suits. He moved again—this time to another town farther down the coast—and bought two German shepherds that he trained as watchdogs.

Up till then Steve had dated gypsy girls almost exclusively, the most recent a sexy, sulky-mouthed brunette named Linda, a year or so older than he was, who came from a Kalderash tribe closely allied with the Bimbos. Night after night they went dancing, which she loved, and she would whisper, "Let's get married. We should be together. You're meant for me. I'm meant for you." The hitch was that she was also firmly wedded to the gypsy tradition. "I'm a money-maker," she said. "I'll make the *boojo,* and I'll fix things up with your father. I already talked to him, your mother too. They want me in the family. We'll go to them just for a couple of weeks, they're in Florida, and you'll see." She even had some older gypsies talk to him.

"If I see Carranza again, I'll kill him," Steve recalls saying.

"Listen to us," one of them said. "If he treats you like before, just have him arrested."

"No, he always gets out."

"But the way you talk you'll do time yourself."

"I don't care. It'd be worth it."

"You're a crazy gypsy boy," he was told. "You think like a *gadjo.* You have their habits."

"I am a *gadjo,*" Steve replied, and as he said this, he saw the shocked look on their faces, almost as if he had uttered some irreversible curse. So he added, "Whatever I am, Carranza made me it. That's who you should be talking to."

Not long afterward he committed the ultimate act of defiance against the gypsy culture by marrying a *gadjo* girl. He had taken up voice lessons and then won a talent-night contest singing in a club on Sunset Boulevard. He devoted every spare dollar and hour he could to the voice lessons and was in still another club hoping to land a singing contract when he met a slender redhead named Ellen. She was sitting with a group of girls when Steve approached her. "I kept smiling at her," he said, "you know, looking at her, and she kept turning her head, so I went over and asked her what she was drinking."

"Nothing."

"Well, I can see you're beautiful. I hope you're not stuck up."

"Did I ask you over here?" she replied.

"No, but let me buy you a drink. Maybe I'm being rude, but you got to excuse me. It's my dumb gypsy manners. I'm a gypsy."

She laughed in disbelief, and he seized on at least this response and said, "It's true. My name's Steven. What's your name? I'm not going to bite you."

"I know, but would you please leave. What does it take to get you to go?"

He persisted. "Listen, if you dance with me, I'll tell your fortune for you," and she laughed again and this time she got up and danced with him.

He went out with her for more than a month, trying to no avail to get her to go to bed with him. She was very secretive about herself. All she would tell him was that she was from Arizona and worked in a store. He would pick her up on a street corner she had designated, and they would go out for dinner and dancing or a movie, and he would return her to the same corner, where she would get out and walk to a parking lot and get into her own car. He didn't try to press her, thinking what difference did it make, that it would all come out in time. While he did not know where she lived, or even her last name, she had his phone number, and after a bitter fight about whether she would ever let him make love to her, she called him several days later and that night they went to a motel. It was very bad; she was tense and trembling throughout, and afterward she said,

"All right, you got what you wanted," and he said, "You don't understand, I love you. I want to marry you."

They drove across the border to Mexico for the wedding ceremony, and she moved in with him. She left each day to work in the store, and he continued with his refinishing business, and at night if he had managed to obtain a singing engagement, she would sit listening to him. Once he asked to see her parents, in Los Angeles, Arizona or wherever they were, and when she refused, he accused her of being ashamed of him, and she denied it, saying that one day she would explain it to him.

In July 1973 she told him that she was pregnant. He was ecstatic at the news. He immediately became concerned about her health and wanted her to quit her job at the store. She said no, that they would need the money more than ever now.

Then, in August, his blissful mood exploded when he got a frantic long-distance call from the youngest of all his sisters. Her name was Susie Tene and she was thirteen years old. She said that their father was selling her into marriage for eight thousand dollars, and she begged Steve to do something to prevent it. He was filled with guilt. He had devoted his energy to his business, the singing and his wife, and this was the first contact he had had with his gypsy family in some time. All the deep-seated anger in him surfaced again, and he promised that he would help her.

His wife said, "You're going to leave me to go back to *them?*"

"It's only for a few days."

"No," she said. "If you go, I'll leave *you.* Stay away from them."

"It's my sister, the youngest," he said. "I have to go."

Short of a wake, there is no social event in the Romany culture like a big wedding. A hall is usually hired, and staggering amounts of food and drink are brought in. One of the ritualistic highlights is the passing around of a huge loaf of bread with holes gouged out in which the guests press gifts of cash; although this money goes to the bride's in-laws, she is expected to steal some of it with mock furtiveness as a harbinger of what she will be doing the rest of her life. The marriage itself takes place when the bride, veiled, appears in her white wedding gown. She also will be wearing perhaps a diamond-encrusted tiara and gold jewelry of one sort or another on temporary loan from her mother-in-law to impress the assemblage. Then she begins an elaborate, flirtatious dance with the groom, each holding one end of a scarf, generally red, that signifies her marital status. Just before the dance a song is traditionally sung by the bride which perversely spells out all the contradictions of gypsy life. On this theoretically joyous occasion the song has her crying out to her mother that she has been sold into marriage, that she would rather die instead, and it ends with a plaintive plea of what should she do? The gypsies consider it moving and beautiful.

On August 22, 1973, his sister Susie's wedding day, Steve Tene arrived at the hall in Boston where the marriage was to take place. There were, he judged, about two hundred Bimbos and allied tribesmen present. He was received icily by the older gypsies, but many of the younger ones greeted him with friendly words and curious stares. Out of the corner of his eye he saw Carranza at a table, already deep in his cups and ignoring him. He asked for his mother and was told that she was helping Susie dress. He was carrying a briefcase, and someone asked him what was in it. "My music," he said. "My sister wants me to sing." Then Susie rushed out in her gown and embraced him.

Holding her hand, Steve, rather than Susie, sang the lament about the bride wanting to die, tears coursing down his cheeks. In the hush that followed, he opened his briefcase and pulled out a .22 pistol. He told Susie to take off the tiara and the jewelry she was wearing, that she wasn't going to get married, that she was coming with him.

Everyone in the hall froze, except his father, apparently too drunk to notice what was happening. Someone said, "Hey, be a nice boy, and put that thing down." His mother suddenly appeared in front of him. He had not seen her in a long time and she seemed weary and on edge. She slapped him.

He pointed the pistol at her. "Bitch!" he said. "How could you do it, selling the youngest like this?"

He saw some of the gypsies circling around him. "Stay away from me," he said, "or you get it." They stopped. Behind them, out of sight, he could hear Carranza cursing. "Let's go," he said to his sister, but she clung to him and said, "Please, Stevie, it's too late. Let me go through with it. He's a nice boy, he'll be good, I think, and if it don't happen with him, it'll happen with someone different. Please, Stevie, please!" She broke away from him and ran into the crowd, sobbing. Later she would explain that it was because she was afraid he would be hurt, possibly killed.

The tension in the hall eased. "You heard her," one of his uncles said. "Your sister wants you to go, so go in a nice way." Steve backed slowly to the door, still holding the gun. He tried one last time. "Susie?" he called. There was no answer, and he went out and jumped into the cab he had waiting for him.

The gypsy custom is that three days must pass before a marriage is consummated, during which time there are a number of additional, smaller parties in honor of the bride and groom. Steve remained in Boston and on the fourth day he went to the house where Susie was, found only her and her mother-in-law at home, and demanded and got the butterfly-bloodstained sheet she had slept on the night before. Full of frustration and anger, he intended to take it to the apartment his parents then had in Philadelphia. He would fling the sheet down before his father. He would have it out with him at last.

When he walked into the apartment, it was as if he had never left. Nothing had changed, and he instantly regretted not bringing his .22 with him. His father was beating Steve's younger brother Tommy for some transgression. The brother just stood there taking it. There was a bloody gash on the side of his head. In a way, Steve thought, it was really worse than ever; Tommy always had been the one offspring that Carranza seemed to spoil. His mother and another sister, Mary, were trying to pull the father away. Then Steve saw his father's ivory-handled revolver on the table. He grabbed it and said, "Leave him alone!"

In his fury Carranza had not seen him come into the apartment. He turned toward Steve and said, "What do you want, you fucking fag?"

"You," Steve said, and thought, well, this is it, I'm going to finish him off for good.

It slowly dawned on the father what was about to

happen, and he moved back. When he got near Steve's mother, he abruptly fell to his knees on the floor behind her, literally hiding behind her skirts. "You can have anything you want," he shouted hoarsely. "Don't shoot. I won't bother you no more. I'll leave you free. I'll leave everybody free!"

Part of his father's immense body was still visible, and Steve moved to one side to get a better angle. He fired. The father screamed. Steve had started to aim the revolver again when his mother, brother and sister were on him, hanging on to his wrist and his hand with the gun. He could see his father bent over, clutching his leg and moaning. Steve suddenly felt as if he were going to throw up. He dropped the revolver and ran out of the apartment.

He returned to Boston. The days and nights slid sickeningly into each other. He drank a lot. He was continuously, exhilaratingly, lightheaded. He couldn't concentrate, could not figure out why he was there. He thought he was going crazy. Then he would remember. It was to watch over Susie. Once he recalled telephoning his wife in California to tell her he would be delayed for a few more days, and she said, "I'm leaving, I've already packed," and he replied, "Don't lie to me like that," and she said, "You're a gypsy, you're back with your family, you're never going to change," and hung up.

On the night of September 7 Steve was drinking in a bar off Tremont Street in downtown Boston. Earlier, in the afternoon, he had been in a gypsy home asking about Susie. The bar he was in was dark and crowded, the jukebox blaring. Someone jostled him, and when he turned, the first fist caught him in the right eye. As he slammed against the bar, he could see out of the other eye that there were two of them, strangers, and then he glimpsed his father standing, watching, by the front door. Another fist got him in the mouth and one in the stomach. He came up, fighting back, and he saw something flashing, a knife, and all at once he could not see out of the left eye either. As he went down, he felt what seemed like stings in his back and vaguely heard a tumult somewhere above him, mixed in with the music, that sounded very far away. After that he passed out.

He was taken to Northeastern University Medical Center. Seven stab wounds in his left shoulder were sutured, as well as two other wounds, one where the knife had sliced into his left temple, and the second under his left lid where it had barely missed plunging into the eyeball itself. His right eye, where he had been first hit, was closed completely, and he was totally, if temporarily, blind. He told the authorities that he had no idea what caused the attack, that it must have been a case of mistaken identity. He gave the hospital the number of a friend he was staying with who came and got him. Three days later the right eye had opened enough for him to see. The eye that had been stabbed was running constantly, and he went to the Massachusetts Eye and Ear Infirmary for treatment. He was given medication and was told that he would continue to have trouble with the eye until the scar tissue was removed.

The next day he flew back to California. When he went into his beach house, it was empty. There was no trace of his wife, no note, not even a hairpin to indicate that she had ever been there. With a gypsy's total unconcern about names, he knew her only as "Ellen" when he dated her, when he married her and when he lived with her. He did know, however, the department store she worked at, near the corner where he used to pick her up, and for three afternoons Steve waited outside for her to appear. She never did. An obstinate pride kept him from going in to make inquiries. Although he cannot read, he had two trunks crammed with papers —insurance settlements, communications from dozens of irate creditors over the years, notes from various people he had met on his travels, storage-room receipts, old airline tickets and the like—and his foster father, sifting through them, finally found her name and number. But when a call was tried, the operator said that the telephone had been disconnected. Steve made no further attempt to locate her, and he has never seen the child.

And now, in the spring of 1974, some seven months after the nightmarish sequence of events that had followed his sister Susie's wedding, Steve had come east again to aid another young sister, Sonia, a near suicide because of Carranza.

After Steve spirited Sonia out of the Bergen Pines hospital in New Jersey and the father swore he would track them down, Steve moved out of the Summit Hotel. He rented a furnished apartment in Manhattan in the East Fifties and nursed his sister back to health.

She told him how she had pleaded with the father not to return her to the husband she had been forced to marry, to let her stay with the gypsy boy she had run off with, and how in desperation she had swallowed a handful of tranquilizers. For five days she remained wan and listless; by the sixth, however, she was acting as if nothing had happened. As I came by to visit them, Sonia was leaning out of the second-floor window, giggling and crooking a finger at me and kidding, "Hey, mister, want your fortune told?" When I expressed my amazement at her transformation, Steve said, "What do you expect? She's a gypsy."

Through the Romany network that seems to work like jungle drums he sent for the boy she loved, who, terrified by the father, had dropped out of sight. Steve was not especially taken by him, but he shrugged and said, "If Sonia wants him, it should be her choice." There remained, however, the problem of the little daughter from her first marriage who was with Carranza and Steve's mother. "He'll never give her up," Sonia said. "He'll hold her over me until I go back." Then late on the afternoon of May 2 Carranza called, even though Steve's number was unlisted. He was in the city, he said, he knew where Steve and Sonia were and he was coming that night to "get" him and take her away.

"All right," Steve said. "I'll be here."

He never came. At about 10 P.M. that night detectives Ray Drago and Frank Bauer of the 102nd Precinct arrested Carranza on an outstanding warrant issued in March in Camden, New Jersey, as a result of a complaint lodged by members of another gypsy tribe with whom the Bimbos constantly feud. As he was being booked, the father tried to con his way out. "Why," he asked the desk officer, "are you doing this to an old man like me?"

There was a hearing in Queens Criminal Court the following day, a Friday, and Carranza was held over the weekend for extradition. After the arrest Steve went to the house in Queens where his mother was still staying, took the little girl and returned her to Sonia. When Sonia, her daughter and her boy friend—really her "husband" now—departed together, Steve told the boy, "Watch out for them. If you don't, you'll curse the day you met me."

There was one last loose end to tie up—the puppy he had found in the trashcan shortly after his arrival in New York. He solved this problem through a secretary he had met one evening while he was searching for Sonia. The secretary's parents had just lost their dog and wanted another one. They were entranced by the puppy at first sight. She told Steve that they had named him "Gypsy." Then he left for Los Angeles. The respite, he knew, was only temporary. Another showdown would come sooner or later.

Throughout the summer the father and son kept up a cat-and-mouse game. After Carranza had been extradited to New Jersey, he posted bond, but neither he nor his accusers showed up for trial, and the case was taken off the court docket. Carranza was reported to be variously in Cincinnati and Cleveland, back in New York, Chicago, next San Francisco and Los Angeles and then New York again. He would periodically phone Steve with renewed threats of vengeance. Before Carranza arrived in Los Angeles, Steve returned to New York to talk to groups of young gypsies, and when his father followed him there, he went to Atlantic City, having realized by now that another confrontation in which he might do something rash would do him no good in the long run. He slipped into New York once more after he learned that Carranza had left for Florida, and Steve was still in New York when the Romany establishment struck back at him.

Around 10 P.M. on September 28, 1974, Steve called me from an apartment in Manhattan. There were three detectives there, he said, who were going to arrest him. He said he was being charged with breaking into an old gypsy woman's home and trying to rob and kill her.

The detectives were from the 68th Precinct in Brooklyn. I spoke to one of them, Nels Nilsen. I told him that I had been interviewing Steve about gypsy life, that a number of gypsies knew of this and were very unhappy about it—indeed, some of them had contacted me to voice their indignation in pretty strong language—and that in addition Steve was involved in a complicated power struggle with certain elements of his tribe. The net result, I said, was that I believed that these charges had been made merely to harass him.

"What we're talking about here," Detective Nilsen said, "isn't harassment. They're very heavy felonies."

"Well," I said, "to the gypsies, that's harassment." The fact that Nilsen said he was acquainted with two books I had written, *The Valachi Papers* and *Serpico,* was helpful. I told him that whatever the facts of the case ultimately turned out to be, I was certain Steve would not skip town until the matter was resolved one way or another. Nilsen decided to let Steve come in on his own the following week. Otherwise, in the normal course of events, he would have been arrested on the spot, booked and held in custody for what remained of the weekend; he would have been arraigned and, in light of the accusations against him, held in substantial bail, perhaps five thousand dollars. If he could not raise the bail, he would have been remanded to the Brooklyn House of Detention for at least three days for a preliminary hearing. If it were found that there was reasonable cause to believe he had committed the crimes he was charged with, he would be bound over for a grand jury appearance. And if he were indicted, a new warrant would be issued, and he would be held for trial.

I was getting enmeshed in gypsy affairs far more than I had bargained for, but I was also being given a chance to observe at first hand the way gypsies will use the criminal justice system for their own purposes. I soon learned that Detective Nilsen, considered an exceptionally savvy law officer, had been bothered right from the start by something in the case, quite aside from my conversation with him. When he first went to see the complainant against Steve, a Mrs. Rosanna Lohr, in her home, he discovered that she kept a dog, a vicious animal which until restrained nearly took Nilsen's leg off while he was questioning her, and she had no ready explanation of why the animal had been so quiet the night of the alleged entry by Steve.

According to Rosanna Lohr, she was asleep in her room about 11:30 P.M. on September 20, a Friday, when she was awakened by Steve, who was "pounding on her chest." With him were two other men unknown to her, one white, twenty-five to thirty years old, with dark hair, the other, also white, about nineteen or twenty, with red hair. Mrs. Lohr stated that she started screaming and called upon Steve to stop. She swore that Steve demanded to know where her late husband's money was. She said that she did not know what he meant by this. She added that she was gravely ill, a victim of cancer, and that because of this she had a companion in the apartment who cared for her and who was sleeping in another room. She called to the companion for help, whereupon Steve and those with him ran off. Mrs. Lohr's companion, one Anne Vlahor, initially corroborated her statement, declaring that she was asleep in the dining room when a male with red hair woke her, pointed a gun at her and told her not to move. She heard Mrs. Lohr scream and cry out "Steve!" and the red-haired male immediately left. The apartment where the entry was supposed to have taken place was on the first floor of a two-story house; the exterior doors were locked, but a window in the kitchen in the rear, approximately six feet above the ground, was open.

The felonies Steve was being charged with were classified as "heinous" crimes on a level just below murder and arson. One was burglary in the first degree; it differs from simple burglary, which is entering premises without permission or authority with the intent to commit a crime, in that it involved a dwelling, it occurred at night when the inhabitants were likely to be present and the perpetrator, as they say, was armed. A second charge was attempted robbery in the first degree because Steve had allegedly threatened Mrs. Lohr with bodily harm in demanding the money. The third, which speaks for itself, was possession of a weapon with intent to use it, in this instance a gun. It seemed

as if it had all been carefully figured out in advance;
Steve, if convicted, faced twenty-five years in prison
and any possibility of his succeeding King Tene as the
tribal chieftain would be dramatically terminated.

I spoke to Steve on the phone the day after his
visitation from the detectives. I asked him where he
had been the night he was supposedly breaking into
Mrs. Lohr's home, and he said in a resigned tone
that he could not remember, that he thought he was
out bar-hopping, but that he really couldn't pinpoint
his movements. I berated him for his lack of memory
and told him that he had better start remembering the
night in detail, that it was important. The fact that he
could not recollect where he had been, however, re-
inforced my belief that he was innocent; if he had
actually pulled off something like this, I was sure that
he would have worked out a well-rehearsed alibi by
now. I then called Charles J. Hynes, one of the top
men at the time in the Brooklyn district attorney's
office. While I knew Hynes only slightly, his reputation
among reporters and law-enforcement officials was that
of a tough-minded but fair prosecutor. I sketched out
the situation with Hynes, as I had with Detective
Nilsen, and told him that although I obviously could
not swear to it, I felt strongly that Steve was being
framed. I asked that he assign one of his most capable
assistant district attorneys to the case, and he agreed
to do so. But when I advanced my theory that Steve
was probably not guilty because he had no alibi, all
I got was a noncommittal grunt. I next contacted Eddie
Coyne, the police department's gypsy expert, and asked
him if he had ever heard of a Rosanna Lohr. Coyne

said that he had, and that on two or three occasions over the last few years he had processed complaints from her that she never followed through on. These complaints, as Coyne said, were typical of the way one gypsy would try to cause trouble for another, and I passed this information on to Hynes.

Things continued to look up a few days later when Steve phoned triumphantly to say that he had finally remembered where he was the night in question. He had been, he said, in a Manhattan bar on Fifty-third Street off First Avenue when the break-in allegedly took place. He had already been in touch with the bartender to confirm his presence there and was busily tracking down some other patrons he had talked to that night. He had recalled the night because it had been raining heavily.

Possibly because of the unexpected investigation of the charges by the young assistant district attorney assigned to the case, Alex Spizz, Mrs. Lohr's companion and corroborator backed away from some of her earlier specific statements and now could no longer remember much more than that something had happened in the apartment that night, quite what she wasn't sure. Rosanna Lohr, however, stuck to her story, and after Steve had been booked and arraigned, she appeared as a witness at the preliminary hearing. Clearly she intended to follow through on the charges.

Her determination was out of character with the complaints Coyne had remembered her making in the past, and I pressed Steve again about who she was. Up till this point Steve had described her merely as a "mean old woman," but now he added, as if it were common knowledge, that she was his "Aunt Rose Bimbo"—the same Rose Bimbo, it would later turn out, who had been in the middle of King Tene's feud with Queen Millie Marks in Chicago some fifty years ago, who had been involved in the Methuen riot and who had been the key witness in the false charges Tene had engineered against King Steve Kaslov in New York in 1932.

At the preliminary hearing, as Rosanna Lohr, she gave her age as sixty-four, but she looked at least ten years older than that, and it was practically impossible to picture her as the raven-haired, willful beauty she once was. She was wearing a long black dress that reached to her ankles and a black shawl. She was short and fat, her face sallow and shrunken; she shuffled forward as if each step were going to be her final one, and she spoke in a faint, quavering voice that could scarcely be heard. She was, I thought, exactly the last kind of witness I would want to have testifying against me.

On the stand, after explaining how she had been awakened from sleep by Steve, gun in hand, she stated, "And I kept on saying, 'Please don't hit me because you know I am dying in the bed. What do you want from me?'"

Asked whom she had been talking to, she replied, "Steve. There was another fellow with him, three fellows altogether."

"Did Steve say anything to you?"

"He said, 'Give me your husband's money.' I begged him not to take it. He says, 'Give me your husband's money.'"

Always on the verge of outright sobs, she told how Steve had punched her in the stomach and on the breast despite the fact that she was suffering from cancer and was on her "dying bed." She threw in some additional color. "He was dancing and singing while he was hitting me," she testified, "and he had the gun in his other hand."

Steve was released on parole pending possible grand jury action, and almost immediately things darkened for him. Records of the previous complaints his aunt had made had been destroyed, since she had not pursued them, so there was no physical evidence to back up this pattern of behavior on her part. There were, of course, certain weaknesses in her story—the inexplicably docile dog on the night of the break-in and also a claim that Steve had made so many threatening phone calls, before actually coming to the house, that she had installed a recorder, but she could not produce any tapes with his voice on them.

All of this paled into insignificance, however, when assistant district attorney Spizz discovered that Steve's alibi did not hold up. Steve had found not only the bartender but also three patrons who swore that they had seen Steve in the bar on a Friday night in September when there had been a heavy downpour. The only problem, as Spizz learned after checking with the weather bureau, was that on Friday night, September 20, it had not rained in New York. There is nothing more irresistible, or convincing, to a prosecutor than a defendant who offers a phony alibi, and as Spizz would later tell me, on the basis of this he was determined to push for an indictment.

I felt largely responsible for Steve's shaky, perhaps perilous, position. I had castigated him so severely about not recalling what he had been doing the night of the supposed break-in that I might have forced him into an explanation, any explanation, of his whereabouts. As it turned out, it had rained heavily on a Friday night in September, but it was the thirteenth and not the twentieth; and as things then stood, it appeared that he would have been a lot better off saying that he could not remember where he was and letting it go at that.

The Bimbo elders, however, in their anxiety to teach Steve a lesson and put him behind bars, went too far when I received a call from San Francisco. A Tom Tene, identifying himself as a relative of Pete Bimbo, said that he knew I had been interviewing Steve, whom he described as a "fucking faggot" and a "dope addict" to boot, and that he and other members of the tribe were ready to step forward to give me a true version of gypsy life. Tom Tene then reeled off the names of a number of gypsies he said were "very upset" that Steve was talking to me. Among them he included Rosanna Lohr. What interested me about this was that he did not mention anything about the break-in as a reason for her anger.

I reported this conversation to Charles Hynes, whom I had first contacted in the Brooklyn D.A.'s office, and asked if Steve and Rosanna Lohr could be given lie-detector tests which, while not admissible in court, would at least give the prosecution an idea of who was telling the truth. Hynes brought me in to see the district attorney himself, Eugene Gold. I related the conversation I had had with Tom Tene, and Gold said that if I could get Tene to repeat what he told me so that it could be taped, a lie-detector test would be in order "in the interests of justice." The D.A.'s office provided a recorder, and in another talk I had with Tom Tene, he repeated what he had said to me in his earlier call, and even though I gave him every opportunity to refer to the break-in, he did not touch on it at all.

As a result Steve was given three tests by a police polygraph expert and, I would later learn, passed "with flying colors." When Alex Spizz, the assistant in tactical charge of the case, asked Rosanna Lohr to take a test too, she refused. And for the first time Spizz noticed a tone of asperity in her normally weak and aggrieved voice. She said she was too sick to come to his office, and when he offered to send a squad car, she still declined and curtly added that she was so sick she was thinking of dropping the charges. But none of this was conclusive, and Spizz, while no longer insisting on an indictment, felt that the matter should be placed before the grand jury with the district attorney's office adopting a neutral stance.

About two months had elapsed since the original complaint was brought against Steve, and some of the gypsies hostile to him, apparently feeling that the case was not moving fast enough, decided to take more direct action. He was always convinced he had been followed the night of the alleged break-in to make sure he was not with friends who could attest that they were with him, and shortly after midnight on December 2, again alone, he came out of a bar and was

walking toward a secondhand car he had purchased
when he heard someone in another car, a white
Cadillac parked in the street, call out, "Hey, Bimbo,
come here."

He could see several figures in the Cadillac, and
the use of the word Bimbo meant they could only be
gypsies. Steve had been living with some friends in
Queens, and he began running toward his own car,
started it and took off along First Avenue on Manhattan's East Side, the Cadillac behind him. When he
reached Fifty-ninth Street, he turned west. This time
it *was* raining heavily, and after proceeding about a
half-block, hoping to lose the Cadillac, he swerved
up a side entrance leading to the lower level of the
Queensboro Bridge. But when he was on the bridge,
the Cadillac was still following him and gaining. There
was not much traffic at that hour, and suddenly the
Cadillac was right behind him and then it was bumping
into him. At each bump, Steve's car skidded on the
wet steel grating that forms a good deal of the bridge's
roadway and he fought to control the car. But when he
managed to do so, there would be another bump and
another skid, each one worse than the last. The Cadillac had much more power than his car had, and after
each bump it easily caught up to him again. The
Queens side of the bridge has several exits separated
by steel pillars supporting its upper level, and as Steve
was approaching them, the Cadillac bumped into him
again, then pulled up alongside and bumped into his
left front fender. He went into another skid; the car
was now out of control and wrapped itself around one
of the steel pillars.

There was one witness to what had happened, a cab driver coming off duty from his company's garage in Queens near the bridge. He had seen that the other car was white, but in the rain he could not make out the license number, although he was certain it was not a New York plate. The cab driver pulled Steve, dazed and bleeding, out of the car and wanted to take him to a hospital. But Steve insisted that he was all right, gave him the address he was going to and asked the cabbie if he would mind taking him there.

When Steve was being helped into the apartment, he realized that he had lost his wallet with a list of important phone numbers in it. One of his friends went to the bridge to see if it was in the car. There were flashing lights from a police car attached to the 108th Precinct as the friend arrived at the scene of the crash. He gave the cops a number where Steve could be called, as well as the name of the cab driver, and found the wallet in the car just before it was towed away. The car was a total wreck, and it was miraculous that Steve had survived. His only injuries were a gash in his forehead at the hairline, requiring eighteen stitches, and a separated shoulder. With so little to go on, there was not much the police could do.

After his recovery Steve still had to go before a Brooklyn grand jury to face the charges brought against him by Rosanna Lohr, also known in various police files as Rose Bimbo, Rose McGinnis, Peggy Fisk, Dorothy Fiske and Anna Pienton. By then I had learned of her past involvement in the affairs of the Bimbo tribe and further discovered that she had been sentenced in 1937 to fifteen years in the Reformatory for Women at Framingham, Massachusetts, and had actually served twelve years of her term. The charge for which she had been convicted was "larceny by trick," and it struck me that this was an extraordinarily harsh sentence for such a crime and that there must have been some reason for it. There was. Rose had enticed a Caucasian woman named Linda Cheng, the wife of a Chinese doctor in suburban Boston, into a *boojo* swindle. Just as Mrs. Cheng was about to hand over $3,580, she had a change of heart and tried to keep the money. Rose and a man she was living with, Charles Pienton, savagely beat her and took the cash anyway. The beating was so brutal that the Boston police made it a matter of top priority and managed to track down the pair in Indiana, four months later.

I relayed this information, along with the pertinent documents, to assistant district attorney Spizz, who indicated that the grand jury would be apprised of it. Rosanna Lohr then testified without any idea that her past activities might be brought up. There was no reason for her to suspect they would be. As gypsies are well aware, when a charge is made, the prosecution does not as a rule look into the complainant's background. That is something the defendant or his attorney is supposed to bring out upon being tried, and in Steve's case it is questionable whether this would have occurred, since he knew nothing about the specifics of her past record. The grand jury, after listening to the evidence, voted not to indict him. Since these proceedings are secret, Spizz would not tell me what took place, but he did reveal that Rosanna Lohr in the witness room before her appearance blurted out the truth of what this was all about when she said, referring to Steve's father Carranza, "My brother should be the rightful king."

With Steve's vindication, I thought that this would be the end of the matter. But I had deluded myself. I was still thinking like a *gadjo*—that there was a beginning, a middle and an end to things. For the gypsies, however, there is no such progression, life is circular, always doubling back on itself, and there is really no end. And immersed in helping Steve defeat the attempt to frame him—together with my concern over the near-miss in trying to kill him—I had forgotten this essential Romany truth, that while most of mankind is at least under the illusion of moving forward, possibly toward its own destruction, the gypsy remains caught in a constant repetitive cycle, not like some primitive society that anthropologists find in, say, some remote valley in the wilds of New Guinea, but in and around bustling, modern, theoretically civilized metropolitan centers.

I had forgotten not only that the gypsies today are still enveloped in the same customs, taboos, feuds and attitudes that they had brought with them in their first great migration across the Middle East centuries ago but also that my own personal involvement with them had an identical rhythmic ebb and flow—that Sonia's forced sale into marriage, her suicide attempt and rescue by Steve could easily have taken place in the Middle Ages; that Rose Bimbo could try to frame Steve Tene in practically the same fashion that she had tried to frame King Steve Kaslov forty-two years before; that the struggle between Steve and his father Carranza mirrored perfectly the violence which was King Tene's true legacy.

I felt that I had come full circle when, almost a year to the day after I had helped Steve slip Sonia out of a hospital in New Jersey, he called me to say that Carranza had once again tracked her down, this time in Los Angeles, and he needed money to get her out of the city. I had even forgotten that, despite all his efforts at emancipation, he too was a gypsy. First he had borrowed my raincoat to get her to safety; now he was borrowing seven hundred dollars. And it occurred to me that this self-perpetuating, totally self-absorbing internal tension was the glue that held the Romany world together and apart from the rest of us.

After his call I went out to see the old *boojo* woman, Aunt Hazel. I found her sitting by the front window of her house, keeping an eye on the neighborhood. As usual, she was aware of everything that had taken place, and I asked her what she thought would finally happen between Steve and his father. "Well," she said in the tone of a fateful philosopher, "seeing is believing. If Stevie can do what he says, being the king, and bringing schooling to our people, educating them, and making things better, the sacrifice of one life ain't so much."

The life she was talking about, of course, was Steve's.

She sighed heavily, her eyes focused somewhere in the occult distance, as if brooding over the inevitability of it all.

Finally I broke the silence. "Aunt Hazel," I said,

"what about the gypsies? What's going to happen to them?"

She seemed startled by the question. "The gypsies?" she said. "Oh, well, we'll just go on, you know, like always."

ABOUT THE AUTHOR

PETER MAAS, forty-eight, grew up in Redding, Connecticut. A graduate of Duke University, he is the author of two previous critically acclaimed bestsellers, *The Valachi Papers* and *Serpico,* both which have been made into major motion pictures. Mr. Maas lives in New York.

WE DELIVER!
And So Do These Bestsellers.

Bantam Book Catalog

Here's your up-to-the-minute listing of over 1,400 titles by your favorite authors.

This illustrated, large format catalog gives a description of each title. For your convenience, it is divided into categories in fiction and non-fiction—gothics, science fiction, westerns, mysteries, cookbooks, mysticism and occult, biographies, history, family living, health, psychology, art.

So don't delay—take advantage of this special opportunity to increase your reading pleasure.

Just send us your name and address and 50¢ (to help defray postage and handling costs).